FROM THE HORSE'S POINT OF VIEW

FROM THE HORSE'S POINT OF VIEW

A Guide to Understanding Horse Behavior and Language with Tips to Help You Communicate More Effectively with Your Horse

Debbie Steglic

From the Horse's Point of View: A Guide to Understanding Horse Behavior and Language with Tips to Help You Communicate More Effectively with Your Horse

Printed in the United States of America

First Printing, 2019

ISBN 978-0-578-60246-2

Debbie Steglic
2010 Black Canyon Rd
Ramona, CA 92065
(619)787-1727
cowgirldebbie@sbcglobal.net

www.cowgirldebbie.com

Credits

Kimerlee Curyl Fine Art

Front cover photo, chapter header photos for Chapters 7, 12, and 13.

Mike Steglic

Interior photos and chapter header photos for Acknowledgments, and Chapters 4, 5, 8, 9, 11, 12, 14, 15, 17, 18, 19, and Closing.

Kathy Ziegler

Introduction header photo and back cover photo.

The remaining chapter heading photos are courtesy of Pixabay.com.

Speculations Editing (speculationsediting.com)

Copyediting: Janell & Alan Robisch

Interior Book Design & Book Cover Design: Janell Robisch

Contents

Acknowledgments i

Welcome iii

Introduction 1

CHAPTER 1 Herd Behavior and Horse Language 7

CHAPTER 2 All Horses Have Individual Personalities 13

CHAPTER 3 The Horse's Photographic Memory and Vision 25

CHAPTER 4 How Horses Learn 35

CHAPTER 5 Is Your Horse in a Learning Frame of Mind? 41

CHAPTER 6 Signs of Tension and Relaxation in Your Horse 45

CHAPTER 7 Reactive versus Responsive Horses 53

CHAPTER 8 Greeting and Haltering Your Horse 63

CHAPTER 9 Saddling Your Horse and Recognizing and Solving Saddling Problems 69

CHAPTER 10 Whoever Controls the Movement of the Herd's Feet Is the Leader 79

CHAPTER 11 Using Phases of Pressure to Accomplish a Task 85

CHAPTER 12 Training Techniques for Confident and Unconfident Horses 91

CHAPTER 13 How to Help Your Horse Become More Confident 99

CHAPTER 14 How Your Emotions and BodyEnergy Affect Your Horse 109

CHAPTER 15 Balancing Leadership Skills, Love for Your Horse, and Communication . . 119

CHAPTER 16 Learned Behaviors 125

CHAPTER 17 Strategies to Help You Gain Confidence with Horses 131

CHAPTER 18 Using Tools 139

CHAPTER 19 Plans, Patterns, Tasks, and Body Energy 147

CHAPTER 20 Safety Tips 155

Closing 163

Acknowledgments

I am extremely grateful to my wonderful husband, Mike, who has stood by me and encouraged me through every step of my horsemanship journey. When I told him my idea for writing this book, he encouraged me and took me to get a laptop to help me get started. After I finished with my rough draft, Mike also did the first leg of the editing. I don't know where I would be without his love and support. I love you with all my heart, Mike.

I am grateful for Parelli Natural Horsemanship and their program for horse lovers. They opened my eyes and heart to a love of learning and natural horsemanship. Because of Parelli, I am a better horsewoman, wife, mother, daughter, sister, and friend. It truly is a self-development program. I had some wonderful Parelli instructors that I was very blessed to work with during my journey through the Parelli program. One of those is Dave Ellis. Thank you, Dave, for all that you have taught me throughout the years. You have been instrumental in my success. Your Parelli clinics and words of wisdom will be with me forever. I also want to thank Margit Deerman for all the fabulous lessons that she has given me throughout the years. Margit has helped me fill in the gaps and kept me growing in my horsemanship journey. I always showed up to our lessons with a list of questions for her to answer, and she filled in all the missing pieces. I am deeply grateful for all that Dave and Margit have taught me. They have enriched my journey in countless ways. Thanks to both of them, I am a better person. Saying thanks just does not seem to be enough.

I also have some wonderful horses of my own and horses that belong to friends and students that have taught me how to be the leader that they needed and deserved. I owe a heartfelt thanks to all of them. They will live in my heart forever.

Finally, my dear friend, Deb Fetherston, was eager to take a peek at my book before it went to the editor. It was great to have a knowledgeable horsewoman's eyes on my book. She helped me to fine-tune several ideas to help you all understand what I was trying to say. Thank you, Deb, for your friendship, love, and support.

Welcome

///

I t gives me great pleasure, through this book, to help you learn how to understand your horse's nonverbal language, gestures, and behaviors so you can communicate effectively with them. When you learn how horses communicate with one another and adjust your nonverbal body language, gestures, and energy to communicate back in a similar manner, you can begin to create a two-way conversation that makes sense to the horse.

It is important to know when a horse is in the right mind-set to learn or to be ridden and when a horse is nervous, reactive, dull, or unresponsive and why. As a horseperson, you need to know what to do to help your horse achieve positive change so that learning and improvement can take place. I want the horse to be confident in our world, and I want you to have the knowledge you need to help your horse gain the confidence he needs so that your relationship can improve and your goals can be achieved.

My hope for this book is to help you become more successful on your horsemanship journey. Being able to effectively understand your horse and knowing how to appropriately communicate with your horse will help you with various problems that you may encounter, such as poor ground manners, impulsion issues, spooking, trailer loading, and saddling. I am here to help you understand what the horse is trying to communicate to you. This information will enable you to give the horse what he needs so that he can give you what you need.

When you are working with horses, there is no one answer to a problem or challenge. Every horse is different, and we have to adjust our strategies and techniques to fit the individual horse. In this book, I offer some strategies that I have found to be useful. It is very important to choose strategies that help your horse gain confidence in himself and in you as his leader. Choosing bad strategies can make horses fearful and unconfident. This leads to negative effects on the relationship you have with your horse. My goal is to help you make choices that are good for the well-being of your horse and the partnership that you share with the horse.

HAPPY HORSEMANSHIP!

Introduction

Ihave always enjoyed watching horses. Anytime I am in the presence of horses, I can't help but focus my attention on them. I have even stopped on the side of the road to watch them interact with one another in a pasture. I find it fascinating to just stop and observe. Decades ago, I found myself watching herds of horses and trying to figure out who was who in the herd, who was the alpha, and what they were trying to communicate to one another, and I also enjoyed watching the foals play and trying to discern what was acceptable behavior and what was not. I could just sit and watch them for hours.

I thought that their language was so simple and easy to understand at the time. After all, if they were excited, they would run and whinny, and their heads and tails would be high. If they were calm, they would graze, relax, or walk casually. I remember thinking that if their tail was swishing back and forth, it meant that they were happy, just like a dog. I thought it was simple and uncomplicated.

Then, when I was in my midtwenties, I got my first horse. He was this beautiful, tall mustang gelding that had the colors of a palomino paint, and he was full of energy, fear, and distrust. He had been rounded up as a yearling in 1988 or so and had the misfortune of being started by an old cowboy who started horses the old cowboy way. After being caught, he had been saddled and cinched up with very little preparation, and he must have been scared to death.

A couple of years after I had purchased him, I was told that the first time that he had been saddled, he'd started bucking, sending the saddle straight up into the air. He'd kicked the saddle two times before it hit the ground! If I had known this, I might have changed my mind about purchasing him.

I named this horse Flaxy and was so intimidated by him that I had to have him delivered to me when I bought him because I did not know how to handle him. Needless to say, I had no business getting a horse that I did not know how to handle. All I saw was that he was so beautiful that I had to have him. It did not take me long to realize that I knew very little about horses, how they thought, or how to communicate effectively with them. This is when my real journey began.

For the next few years, I barely got by with this lack of horse knowledge. I figured that everybody who had owned a horse longer than I had must have known more about horses than I did. I was hungry to know more, and I sought advice from anyone at the boarding stables who would listen to me. I had tons of questions, and I was determined to learn. I knew how to stay on a horse, and we could ride on the trail pretty successfully. For the time being, I was OK with that, although I did keep searching for answers to my basic questions, such as how to keep my horse out of my personal space when I was leading him somewhere and how to teach him to back up.

All the other people around me demonstrated a shocking lack of knowledge as well. Nobody seemed to know how to fix the problems I was having. How could there be so many people with horses that did not know how to resolve their own issues?

I had several dreams where Flaxy and I were together and he would start communicating with me in English. I was so shocked and happy that he could talk and told him that I had so many questions. I wanted to communicate with him so much. I wanted to understand him.

I had two things going for me at the time: determination and a lack of fear. At least at that time, I thought those were good. As it turned out, my lack of knowledge and my lack of fear did not serve me well. After several years with Flaxy, I still lacked knowledge, but I was pretty confident about riding on the local trails. Then the day came when a friend was having trouble with his horse during a trail ride, and I thought I could fix it. I dismounted, walked confidently over to his horse, and began to immediately get on. As I put my foot in the stirrup and began to swing my other leg over his back, he reared up, terrified, flipped over backward, and landed on top of me, saddle and all, on the asphalt. I woke up in the hospital with a concussion, and as a result of the encounter, I permanently lost my sense of smell.

The accident turned my whole life around. Fear crept in, and my riding took on a lack of confidence. What I was about to learn really shocked me. The more unconfident I became, the more unconfident Flaxy became. I tried to hide it and disguise it, but I was not tricking Flaxy at all. The horse that had learned to trust me now was losing that trust. I was not his confident, fearless leader anymore.

I soon found myself at a crossroads. My fear was stronger than ever, and I did not know how to fix it. Then, suddenly, my beloved Flaxy became ill and passed away. I did not know what to do. My love for horses was so strong, but so was my fear. *What do I do?* I asked myself. *Do I walk away from horses and leave my fear with them? How can I get another horse when I have lost my confidence with them?*

As it turned out, I could stay away from the stables for only a couple of days after losing Flaxy before I had to go back. I missed my best friend Flaxy more than words could say, but I also missed just being around horses. A couple of days away seemed like a lifetime. I was like a magnet being drawn back to the stables. I knew then that I would have to get another horse.

I started searching and found the same thing over and over again: horses that were dull and resistant. Many looked like they just did not have a zest for life anymore. At the time, my budget was small, and I could not afford a well-trained, well-bred horse. Then I met a new friend at the stables who had a very nice mare that she was willing to lease me for riding and breeding. So, if I could not find a horse for sale that I liked, I could just breed a mare and start from scratch

Since I still lacked knowledge, this brought on a whole other set of challenges. I had visions of this future foal that I could imprint, love, and handle with such care that the horse would be almost like a big puppy dog, and we would have this amazing relationship. I envisioned us galloping around everywhere together, and she would be so attuned to me that we could accomplish anything. What a beautiful dream! I had it all worked out in my mind. It was going to be amazing. No more fear, just blissful fun.

Then came the day when she was born. I had stayed in a camper right next to the stall so that I could be present for the birth. I called my friends so they could be there to witness it and help with the imprinting. We were all so excited. The birth went well, and she was beautiful. She had a perfect blaze down her face and a nice sorrel coat, and she was beautiful. My heart was filled with love, and my dream had arrived. My friends and I had practiced some imprinting techniques on dogs so that we would be prepared, and we even made a big poster with all the information for imprinting on it so that we would not forget anything. We were set, and we were going to rock this first session with the newborn foal, whom I had named Cheyenne.

That moment was short-lived. Cheyenne's dam rejected her immediately after birth. Her mom squealed, kicked at her, and completely panicked. It was several hours before Cheyenne's dam would allow her close enough to nurse, and the two needed to be monitored for quite a while after that to make sure that Cheyenne did not get hurt.

We proceeded with the imprinting, but we did not have enough savvy at the time to realize that we were not doing it correctly. None of us really understood the concept at that time, so instead of conditioning her to relax when we added stimulus, we taught her to tense up. If you stop a stimulus when a horse is still nervous, worried, or scared, the horse will continue to have that same response. So, our well-intended plans all backfired.

Cheyenne turned out to be a complex individual from the first day. I did not understand how to be the leader that she needed me to be. All I wanted to do was to love her, play with her, and eventually ride off into the sunset with her. Cheyenne would not have any of that. She was fearful, untrusting, defiant, introverted, and often hard to figure out. She would not let me love on her, and she was mentally and emotionally braced against me.

Cheyenne turned out to be one of my greatest teachers. It was because of her that I went on a quest to learn as much as I could about horses and horsemanship. I did not know it at the time, but this would also lead me on a quest of self-development. I found out that I couldn't have one without the other, that horsemanship and self-development go hand in hand.

There is a saying that your horse is your mirror. Cheyenne reflected back to me that I had a lot of self-work to do. In her first few years, she kicked me, bucked me off, and even came up behind me and bit me aggressively on the calf muscle. Luckily, I had jeans on. Someday, I may have to write a book just about our journey together.

Cheyenne is still with me, and she is eighteen years old now. We have come a long way together, and I have been able to accomplish a lot with her over the years. She is now light and responsive and has beautiful gaits.

Today, she is retired and lives in a pasture with my other horses. She is not sound enough to do much with anymore, and she has had some slips and falls out in the pasture, which have left her with injuries. However, our relationship is good, and she comes to me regularly with a soft, gentle expression on her face. She has always been the alpha with every horse I have had her with. No other horses have ever been allowed to groom her, but she will allow me to do it without any negative expressions. This is *huge* for her!

As I mentioned, during the trials and tribulations of raising this horse, I began my quest to learn more about horses and how to gain confidence and solve problems. A friend loaned me a DVD of a man named Pat Parelli riding a horse bareback and bridleless around an open field. Together, they were galloping up and down hills, working a cow, spinning, and turning. As I watched, my eyes were huge, and my mouth was wide open. I had never seen such a demonstration. I decided that I needed to find out more. I wanted to be able to do what he was doing. The video gave me hope that I could get my dream back. Soon, I began studying Parelli Natural Horsemanship, and I never looked back.

That does not mean that the journey was easy. I was challenged in so many ways. In the beginning, I was unconfident, Cheyenne was unconfident, I could not understand her, and she wanted nothing to do with me. I would go out to the pasture to get her, and she would run to the other end of the pasture. It is hard to learn on a horse that is learning too.

In his program, Parelli said that beginners should start with their easiest horse, but I was stubborn. I wanted to learn with Cheyenne, and I made more mistakes than I could possibly count. In time, I learned that this journey was more about my self-development than her horse development. I needed to become humble and be a good student. I needed to learn the horse's language and how to become a horsewoman. My own journey of self-development affected every aspect of my life. I became not just a better horsewoman but a better wife, mother, friend, and teacher.

I ended up having to work my way through the Parelli program with three different horses. I worked my way to Level 3 with Cheyenne, and when she started having soundness problems, I switched to a wonderful quarter horse, who got me through Level 3 and part of Level 4 before arthritis got the best of her. I was then fortunate enough to acquire a wonderful Atwood Ranch appendix horse, whom I named Troubadour. Troubadour and I passed Level 4 together.

With this solid foundation under our belts, I decided I needed to do something with it. I looked into many sports and decided that I wanted to try cowboy dressage. I liked the principles behind the sport because I felt that they matched up with my own, so I gave it a try.

Our first time competing was nerve-racking for me. I was nervous, and this made Troubadour nervous. When he saw the judging booth, he spooked and became very tense. Needless to say, we did not score well.

After our first initiation into the competition world, things got much better. I decided to compete in the two hardest tests offered at the time in the Cowboy Dressage Open Division in Southern California. That year, we entered several competitions, and we scored first or second on every test. We also came home with two ribbons for High Point Reserve Champion and two Champion halters. What mattered to me was not so much the ribbons and halters but the compliments that I got from other riders telling me how beautiful it was to watch me and Troubadour ride together. Our harmony and connection were noticed.

I wanted people to see that they could achieve their dreams with a horse without force and tie downs and that their relationships with their horses could be harmonious.

I will always continue to learn and grow as a person and a horsewoman. I love studying and playing with the art of finesse riding, bridleless riding, liberty work, and cowboy dressage and will continue to expand my interests. I also love to teach horsemanship, and I love to help people to understand their horses so that they can achieve their dreams. The journey will never be over for me. It is my love and passion, and in this book, I hope to share it with you.

CHAPTER 1
Herd Behavior and Horse Language

Understanding horse behavior, how horses naturally interact with one another and with their environment, is an important first step in learning how to understand and communicate with horses. Horses, even with their large size, are prey animals, and it is natural for them to be reactive and flee from perceived danger. Horses communicate with the other horses in the herd with mostly nonverbal language. A horse that is worried about potential danger might alert the other horses by raising his head and tail and snorting. These actions alert the other horses and prepare the herd to flee. The horse's language is made up of mostly nonverbal language and gestures. Everything that the horse needs to communicate with other horses, including his emotions, is expressed with these tools.

One of the horse's instincts is to push into pressure. This tendency can be seen in acts such as one horse fighting for a dominant position in the herd or two stallions fighting over mares. Each horse involved in the dispute will try to persuade the other to back away by applying pressure. He may begin with negative expressions, such as pinning back his ears, wrinkling his nose, or swishing his tail, to tell the other horse to move away or back down. If this does not work, biting, rearing, and kicking will come into play until one of the horses backs away from the pressure. The horse that backs away will lose the battle and be seen as more submissive.

Horses are also fearful of things that are not familiar. Anything unfamiliar may be perceived as dangerous to the horse, especially if the object in question is in motion and moving toward him. On windy days, there are a lot of things moving around; this can make it hard for a horse to detect where danger might be coming from and may leave him feeling nervous. This nervousness can be seen in signs such as a high head, unblinking eyes, twitching ears, snorting, aimless running, and a high tail. With some unconfident, low-energy horses, they may look almost frozen in place, as if they are afraid to move anywhere. In the wild, horses are on constant alert for anything moving around. Even in a pasture setting, horses align themselves in opposite directions to help protect the herd. There could be a hungry mountain lion lurking in the bushes after all. Horses can easily go from a relaxed state of mind, where they graze or rest, to an alert state of mind, where they raise their heads and their adrenaline increases. If they are not ready to flee at a moment's notice, a member of the herd could be killed.

Domestic and wild horses instinctually think in the same way. They feel safer when they are with other horses or when they are with a person that is perceived as a leader. Whether a horse lives in a stall next to other horses or in a pasture with a group of horses, he will be mentally and emotionally in tune with the state of mind of the other horses.

Oftentimes, when a horse is taken away from horses that he lives close to, he will become emotionally unstable and fearful. It is not normal for a horse to be taken away from his herd. It is also not normal for a horse to live in isolation from other horses.

The good news is that when you become a good leader for your horse, it will help your horse feel safer with you and be less dependent on the herd for safety. That said, social interaction with other horses is still important for a horse's well-being. Always take your horse's need for interaction with other horses into consideration when choosing living conditions and stall placement.

Horses love to graze, and wild horses can spend as much as fifteen to twenty hours a day grazing. They can cover many miles a day looking for food and water. The lead mare decides where the herd will go, and the stallion stays at the back of the herd, making sure everyone follows the lead mare. If any horses are not keeping up with the herd, the stallion does whatever is necessary to get those horses back with the herd. The stallion may start off by walking behind the offending horse, pinning his ears straight back, or tossing his head around. If that does not work, the stallion might bite him or kick out at him to let the animal know he is serious. The stallion starts with suggestions and escalates to using further forms of pressure only if the herd member chooses not to respond to the stallion's request.

As horsemen and horsewomen, we use similar escalations of pressure to encourage the behavior we are looking for. We start light and increase pressure only if necessary.

Understanding this herd behavior can help you simulate the roles of the lead mare and stallion when you are interacting with a horse. Asking a horse to execute a certain task is similar to the lead mare letting another horse know what she wants him to do. If there is resistance to your request, you can add some pressure just as a stallion would do to make your horse slightly uncomfortable and think about fulfilling the request. It is also important to understand that there can be many different reasons that your horse does not want to fulfill your request. Understanding the horse's language is key to understanding the reason behind the horse's resistance. The horse may not understand the request, may be fearful or defiant, or may feel that you are lower in the pecking order. He may also be in pain or injured. Before you add pressure to encourage the horse to execute a task, take great care to see whether your horse understands what is being asked of him. Make sure the horse is not acting out of fear but is instead responding respectfully without fear. As you read this book, you will become more familiar with the horse's body language, what the language means, and ways to communicate effectively.

It is important to understand that horses also tune into each other's emotions. If one or more members of the herd feel that there is danger, their adrenaline will come up, and they will raise their heads high. Their nostrils will flair, they may raise their tails, and their eyes may go wide and unblinking. As soon as one horse becomes alert, all the other horses will pick up on those emotions and respond in the same way almost instantly. A decision will be made quickly as to whether the threat is real and they should run away or it is a false alarm and they should come off adrenaline, put their heads back down, and go back to grazing or whatever the herd was previously doing. If the herd does decide that there is danger and it is time to flee, the safest place for an individual is in the middle of the herd, where he is less likely to be the victim of an attack.

The ultimate "herd relationship" is that of a dam and her foal because the foal is so reliant on the dam. When foals are born, they will be up on their feet within a short period of time. This is very important to their survival in the wild because there are predators to watch out for, and they may have to flee at a moment's notice. Foals are also born with their eyes open and the ability to learn very quickly. They rapidly learn who their mother is and who everyone else in the herd is. They also learn all the nonverbal body language and gestures of the horse language and how to conduct themselves within the herd. Everything foals need to know to survive is picked up within a very short period of time. Even a foal that is born in a stall with only his mother to interact with will learn this language. Since foals are such quick learners, it is very important for a horseperson to have more advanced skills before training foals.

People often love to love on their foals. They are so adorable, and they are often treated like big puppies. So, the foal often learns to be pushy with people and wins many dominance games without the people around them even realizing it. For example, foals love to nibble on things and will often take an opportunity to nibble on a person. It does not take long before a nibble can turn into a bite. I find it helpful when I am spending time with a foal and petting him or teaching him something to just make it difficult for the foal to nibble on me. I just make sure that I have an elbow or arm in the way so that the foal runs into my arm and finds that it does not feel so good to try to bite it. The foal gets discomfort instead of pleasure out of the action and so gets no satisfaction out of trying to nibble on me. In the horse's mind, he has chosen not to bite because it was not fun. Alternatively, if an owner chooses to smack a foal for biting, the horse might either become scared and head shy or just learn to be faster at biting next time.

Many foals also love to have their hind quarters scratched, and owners are often happy to oblige. Within a short period of time, such a foal may begin to turn his hind end to the owner, demanding a scratch. Once again, the owner is happy to scratch away. The owner does not realize that the foal is expressing dominance. When the foal turns his hind end to the person, it is similar to a horse turning his butt to another horse to let him know that if he does not move away, he will get kicked. So, the foal begins to feel as if he is the dominant one, and then one day the owner gets kicked and does not understand why.

As foals get older and stronger, they can become increasingly pushy, and this can be dangerous. There is nothing wrong with loving on a foal as long as you do it with the understanding that he is practicing being an adult horse. It is very important to raise your foal to be confident, curious, and respectful as he grows up. Love on the foal, but make sure that he is respectful of you and your space. Allow him to be curious about his new world so he can build confidence. Punishing a foal can cause him to become fearful, unconfident, or aggressive, depending on his personality. It is best to just patiently and lovingly teach him his boundaries. That being said, working with foals while they are young can be very beneficial to their development.

Just as horses are tuned into the emotional states of other horses, they are also tuned into the emotional states of the people around them. If a person is mad, frustrated, or upset, the horse feels that. If a person is scared or unsure, the horse feels that as well. The horse also knows when you are pleased. When you reward his every try and slowly advance his learning, the horse comes out feeling like a confident partner. If you look for the moments when you can reward the horse instead of focusing on his mistakes, he becomes engaged in the process and can become a super learner. If you can recognize when the horse is trying to fulfill a request, you can be ready to either release or soften pressure from him, depending on the situation. This way, the horse can think his way to the right answer. When the horse does fulfill a request and you take the pressure off immediately, the horse understands that he has done the right thing. If you keep the pressure going after the horse has put in effort or fulfilled a request, there will be no way for the horse to understand that he has done the right thing. As you proceed through this book, I will show you the signs to look for to determine when the horse is trying to fulfill a request, when you should be adding pressure to encourage your horse to respond to your request, and when you need to give the horse time to think his way through a situation without pressure.

If you are working on a task or pattern with a horse and you find that he has shown some improvement, stop the task for the day, and let him feel successful. Pet and praise him, and let him relax for a few moments. If you ask the horse to repeat the task again, he will lose enthusiasm because he will feel as if his efforts are not valued. It is important to understand that progress is made in small steps. A little bit of progress each day builds a self-confident horse that trusts you and learns to love learning. If you look at it in human terms, this is no different from you just learning the basic steps to the two-step and the dance instructor immediately asking you to go on the dance floor and add some twirls and spins in front of the class. Your enthusiasm would drop instantly, and you would feel inadequate. Learning comes in advancing one step at a time. You and the horse can work on that same pattern or task later on, but give the horse a break from it for now. If it was a difficult task, go do something else with the horse that is less demanding, such as a trail ride or a simple pattern or task. Alternately, spend some time with the horse without putting any demands on him. It can be very hard to quit a task or pattern when it is going well and the horse is showing improvement. We get excited, and we want more, but if we ask for more, oftentimes, it will get worse because the horse will feel like he is never good enough.

Once you begin to understand your horse's nonverbal body language, gestures, and emotional state, you can start to interact with him in a way that is beneficial for your relationship. When this happens, you can share and understand each other's ideas and points of view. You can also understand what it takes to be a leader for your horse and, with him, learn how to gain mutual respect. A horse that is responding respectfully is one that is positively engaged with you, one that is light, attentive to you, responsive, and willing to please. A horse that is responding out of fear or frustration is one that is emotionally reactive and, therefore, responding negatively to the situation. This horse could become overreactive, physically and emotionally resistant to requests, dull, nonresponsive, or mentally shut down.

When you gain the knowledge and skills to effectively communicate your wishes, the chances of a positive outcome greatly increase. As your ability to be effectively understood by your horse and his willingness to fulfill your requests increase, he will begin to see you as a benevolent leader. This horsemanship will take some time to master but is available to anyone willing to take the time to learn.

I have even seen people in wheelchairs master the art of horse communication and leadership both on the ground and while riding. The key to becoming a better horseperson is to understand the horse language and become aware that the more we develop our own skills and emotional fitness, the better our results will be with our horses. The positive and negative signs to look for are listed throughout this book.

CHAPTER 2
All Horses Have Individual Personalities

Cheyenne, whom I discuss at length in the Introduction, became one of my greatest teachers. She was a complex character who I believe came into my life to help me become a better person and a better horsewoman. I had a hard time figuring out her personality from day one.

In some situations, such as during the time she spent with other horses, she was very dominant, but she would take the leadership role fearfully instead of confidently. Cheyenne became the alpha horse by running around the other horses, kicking out, and fearfully squealing until all the others decided that they did not want to mess with her.

When I worked with her, she would become very concerned about any learning sessions that we had together. I was a student and did not understand how to properly use training techniques with her. At that time, I did not understand that every horse has his own individual personality or that there are different strategies for different personality types. As a result, I used strategies that caused her to lose confidence instead of gain it. As our sessions continued, she became more unconfident, and her behaviors became increasingly worse. This mare and I were struggling together, and my approach was all wrong for her. Cheyenne was unconfident by nature, and her energy would switch from unconfident and low energy to unconfident and high energy in a split second, especially when any pressure was put on her.

One afternoon, we were practicing some riding patterns in the arena. I was adding in lots of transitions between gaits and many turns, and I felt her tension increasing very fast. We were cantering, and she started going faster and faster. As I look back now, I can see that her body was full of tension, and she could not take the pressure anymore. I had been asking way too much of her and was not taking into consideration her emotional state. I did not even understand how to tell when she was worried or concerned because she did not show it outwardly except in moments like this. As Cheyenne continued to pick up speed, I thought it might be a good idea to add some quick changes of direction to get her attention back on me, but all it did was worry her more.

Cheyenne finally could not take the pressure anymore, so she stopped and froze in place. She put her head down close to the ground, and I could not move her, turn her, or do anything with her. Her body was stiff with tension, and her mind had frozen up. I got off her and just watched with complete confusion. It was at this point that I realized that I did not know much at all about horses and that I needed to dig deep and commit to learning all that I could.

Looking back, I realized that Cheyenne did not need more work or more pressure. She needed me to learn how to teach her to become calm and confident so that she would be ready to learn. She also needed me to understand when she was nervous, scared, or unsure of what I expected of her so that I could help her work through it in a way that was appropriate for her. Cheyenne needed me to be able to read the signs that I will share with you in this book. She needed me to take the time to teach her tasks one step at a time and to release pressure at appropriate moments so that she would know when she was doing something right. I needed to be in control of my emotions and be a calm and confident leader. Cheyenne also needed breaks between tasks to process the information from the lesson. Once I began to understand all this, things began to change, and our relationship blossomed.

First, I went on a quest to learn more about horses and their different personalities. I became aware that each horse needed to be treated as an individual, and I learned many strategies to help horses to become confident in learning situations, in different environments, in themselves, and in me as their leader. I began to understand their horse language and how every gesture, expression, and movement meant something. I learned how important it was to interact with them by using the same type of nonverbal communication and body language that they used with one another.

There are many different personality traits that horses have, and in this chapter, I break them down into four different categories that I find helpful in understanding them. This does not mean that a horse will fit into a specific category perfectly because he won't. Horses may show personality traits from different categories, and sometimes, they will react completely differently in different situations. Here are a couple of examples:

- A horse may be low energy, lazy, and self-confident while working in an arena doing routine drills but may then become high energy and unconfident on a trail ride or in a new environment.

- A horse may be high energy and self-confident on a trail ride but may then become high energy and unconfident in a learning situation or in a show ring.

The key is recognizing how a horse is reacting in the present situation and understanding the strategies that will help the horse in that situation. Don't be tricked into thinking that the horse fits into only one category all the time. One of the categories may be the dominant personality trait for a horse, but certain situations may bring out less confidence, more worry, or more dominant behavior. This makes it important for you to understand the different personality traits so that you have strategies to help the horse at any time in any situation. It is a great feeling to be able to recognize when a horse is confident and when he is not and to have strategies to help the horse out in either case.

Next, I list the four different personality traits that I commonly see.

High-Energy, Self-Confident Horse

Some horses have a tendency to be full of energy and self-confidence. They love to run around and have fun. They are very curious about their environment and love to explore and play with other horses and different objects. This type of horse may also be very dominant by nature and be more prone to being pushy and dominant toward other horses and people. This does not mean that he never gets nervous or scared; it just means that this is the behavior most commonly seen with this horse.

High-energy, self-confident horses often

- Love to play
- Love to approach or chase objects
- Are mouthy
- Are pushy
- Are friendly with people
- Are mischievous
- Learn fast
- Get bored with too much repetition
- Challenge authority
- Love to move around a lot
- Move the tail in a soft, flowing motion from side to side when relaxed and having fun
- Swish the tail back and forth fast and tight when feeling irritable or mad

Strategies to Help a High-Energy, Self-Confident Horse Excel

This type of horse benefits from having some variety in whatever sport you engage in to keep him interested and having fun. The confident horse generally learns fast and needs less repetition than the unconfident horse. He still needs you to break down each task and teach him one step at a time, but progress can be accomplished a lot more quickly if he is taught with clarity and fairness, receives a release of pressure when he has responded correctly, and gets lots of praise for his efforts, which helps builds enthusiasm. A release of pressure does not always mean stopping. Sometimes, it means slowing down to a lower gait, a nice pet on the neck, a "good boy" or "good girl," or a momentary loosening of the reins.

This horse does not like to feel drilled, so changing up the routine or patterns you are working on may help him to be more engaged in the activity.

Also, this type of horse may act lazy when he is bored or drilled too much on a certain discipline or task. He may quit trying and then start acting dominant toward you. He may exhibit behaviors such as pushing you around, refusing to go forward, biting, kicking out at you, bolting when he is pushed too hard, or refusing to follow a request.

To avoid boring him, add in some fun, and keep progressing with your learning and teaching. Don't punish him for his personality traits. He is not trying to be bad or mean; he is just full of energy and mischief. If some negative behaviors show up, it is up to you to engage his mind in more progressive activities.

Keep in mind that this horse learns quickly and likes to have fun, so if you have a horse like this, you need to be up for the challenge. Reward him often with scratches, petting, and playful time together. Have some toys, such as a big ball or a small ball with a handle, and maybe some jumps and pedestals to make things more interesting. Use a lot of your own energy and enthusiasm to match his personality. The more positive and progressive you are with this horse, the more mentally and physically engaged he will be.

It is also a good idea to do something different with this type of horse after a few sessions of learning or practicing a sport. This will add some extra variety and make your time together more fun for both of you. Enjoy a trail ride or play a different sport just for fun. If you let the horse burn off some energy before you ask him to focus on a lesson, your chances of success will greatly increase. Have this high-energy, confident horse mentally and physically engaged with you before you ask him to learn something new or improve on a task. If his mind is elsewhere and you are trying to make this horse do something, it probably won't go well.

With the right training and athletic ability, the high-energy, self-confident horse can be great in such jobs as

- Cutting
- Reining
- Ranch work
- Competitive trail riding
- Endurance work
- Jumping
- Working equitation
- Obstacle challenges

High-Energy, Unconfident Horse

Some horses are born with lots of energy but lack self-confidence. This type of horse typically worries a lot, panics easily, and needs to move his feet a lot. This horse may lack self-confidence in learning situations and new environments and be scared of objects that he is not familiar with as well as any changes in his environment. You need to take your time and help this unconfident horse build his self-confidence. At the beginning of a session, it is best to work on getting this horse calm and mentally engaged with you and your requests before you begin working on your sport of choice or teaching new skills. This horse needs you to be confident, knowledgeable, and perceptive to his mental and emotional states and his needs. Reward the horse's every effort, and give him breaks between tasks so that he has time to think and mentally process information.

If you have a high-energy, unconfident horse, he may

- Be quick to bolt
- Have a high head
- Move his ears around a lot
- Have wide, unblinking eyes with visible whites
- Whinny
- Snort loudly or sneeze
- Be overreactive and worried
- Have trouble standing still
- Be spooky
- Be fearful

- Be tense all over his body
- Frantically run around with a high head
- Have a high tail
- Not deal well with punishment or being pushed to learn too fast
- Panic when there is too much stimulus or pressure

Strategies to Help a High-Energy, Unconfident Horse Excel

This horse does not do well when too much pressure is put on him. Be light with your aids and tools when you request something. Start with the lightest amount of pressure possible, and give the horse a few moments to think his way to the correct answer. When the horse is confused and not sure about what your request is, it is important to not add additional pressure; just maintain a light amount. The horse just needs time to think and experiment until he finds the correct step of action. If you find that the horse is not paying attention to you and his thoughts and emotions are elsewhere, you can slowly add more pressure until he begins to respond to your request. It is very important to take away or release the aids, tools, or pressure immediately the moment the horse responds correctly. If pressure is kept on the horse after he has responded correctly, chances are that he will only get worse. If the pressure is not taken off him the moment that he responds appropriately, he will not understand that he has done the right thing, and he will become more worried and fearful.

When this horse is on a lead line, it is also important not to hold it too close to the halter. This prevents the horse from being able to move when he needs to, and he will feel claustrophobic and can panic even more. It is also more dangerous because it keeps him too close to you, and you have a higher chance of being hurt. Give the horse several feet of lead rope so he can move his feet around. Trying to prevent this horse from moving will cause him more anxiety. Walk along with him and direct where his feet should go. Change the direction you are walking often, and stay calm and focused. Often, this will help your horse calm down.

Repetition with patterns can also be calming to a high-energy, unconfident horse. If this horse needs to move his feet, help him by directing where his feet should go. Do your best to keep a level head and not become overactive yourself; this will only make the horse more worried. This type of horse needs confident, calm leadership. Don't just put him in a round pen or arena and let him run around aimlessly. This will not help him to become calm and start thinking again; it can actually make the situation worse. He needs your leadership. Have him go over obstacles such as jumps and ground poles. This will help him think about something other than being worried or panicked. Do lots of patterns, such as figure eights or small circles, including around obstacles, and change directions. Back up the horse until his head lowers. Also, try side passing or leg yields to help him to become more responsive and less reactive. Don't push this horse to do something that he is not confident doing. Get him calm, responsive, and focused on you before trying to teach him something new.

Look for signs of relaxation, such as

- A lowered head
- Ears pointed toward you
- Soft and blinking eyes
- Relaxation in his breathing, normal-size nostrils with no wrinkles, and possibly soft sneezes
- Lip licking
- Rhythm in his gait
- His attention on you

These are all signs that the horse is becoming calmer and more responsive to you rather than reactive and frantic. When you see these signs of relaxation, give the horse a break; let him stand still, and give him time to put his head down, blink, and lick his lips. This will help him release his adrenaline and reflect on his decision to relax.

I will talk more about the importance of these types of breaks for horses in upcoming chapters.

Once the horse has licked his lips, has started looking around, and is more alert, you can start your teaching session. It is best to keep the learning sessions short and remember to reward every effort so the horse can gain confidence. A reward can be a release of pressure, a smile with a verbal "good boy" or "good girl," a treat, allowing him to drop to a lower gait, or even giving him a break. He needs to feel successful so he knows he is doing the right thing. Short and successful learning sessions will help your horse gain confidence. If you want to spend more time with your horse after a learning session, you can go on a trail ride, play a sport that he enjoys, or just casually walk around without asking too much of him. See if your horse wants to roll in a soft area such as an arena. Stay with him while he rolls in the dirt or sand. This way, your horse understands that you do more together than just work. This helps build rapport.

If your horse is worried and you cannot calm him down and have run out of ideas, be sure to quit before you get frustrated or mad. You can always put him back in the stall or pasture and seek more answers. There is no one answer. Every horse is different, and there are lots of positive ways to engage the horse's mind and body. Try not to get mad or frustrated; it will only create more problems and disharmony, and your horse will learn that he can't trust you. You are working toward a future with your horse. Every session is a stepping-stone toward a confident, respectful, and responsive horse that can be your dream partner.

With the right training and partnership, high-energy, unconfident horses can be great athletes and excel in activities such as

- Endurance
- Ranch work
- Dressage
- Working equitation
- Western dressage
- Cowboy dressage

Low-Energy, Unconfident Horse

Some horses are born with a tendency to be naturally skeptical, fearful, and emotionally tense. These horses can often be hard to figure out. They may look calm and relaxed because they are not moving around a lot or showing a lot of outward expression. This type of horse may keep his head low and look as if he is calm. He can be emotionally and physically slow and tense and is often mistaken for a confident, low-energy horse because their outwardly appearances can be very similar.

Learning sessions, new environments, and unfamiliar obstacles can bother this horse. Take your time introducing him to anything new, and help him slowly gain confidence. This horse needs you to be a confident leader that has a plan for your time together. The horse needs you to understand his needs, teach him new tasks slowly and methodically with lots of repetition, and take the time to help him understand and gain confidence.

If you have a low-energy, unconfident horse, he may show the following characteristics:

- A lack of blinking when worried
- Hesitation in responding
- Timidity
- Kicking when afraid
- Being easily spooked
- Fear
- Inward tension
- Natural obedience
- A desire to please you
- Sensitivity about his personal space
- A lot of worry

- Lack of confidence in learning
- Negative responses to punishment, too much pressure, or being pushed to learn too fast
- Mentally and sometimes physically shutting down when there is too much stimulus or pressure

Strategies to Help an Unconfident, Low-Energy Horse Excel

If your horse is more on the fearful side, you may find that he needs more consistency or routine in his training or your specific sport to feel more confident. Horses understand patterns very well, and repeating a pattern can help a nervous horse become a little calmer and relaxed and not worry so much. Patterns, such as riding in circles, a figure eight pattern, a dressage pattern, or a Western or cowboy dressage pattern, or a familiar trail may help your horse feel safer and help him understand what is expected of him.

This horse will also benefit from clear, calm, and confident guidance from you. This will help him build confidence and trust in you as his leader. It will also help if your emotions are calm and you are confident. Take your time teaching tasks to the unconfident horse. Break down each task into small steps, and make sure that the horse understands each step before you add another piece to the task.

Make sure the cues you give when asking an unconfident horse to do something are gentle, light, and consistent. Give this horse time to pause and reflect on a task well done and to just stand still for a few moments. Uninterrupted time to rest and reflect on what the horse has just accomplished will help him process the task or lesson, and it will give his emotions a little break. If you can let the horse rest long enough for him to sneeze, do some blinking, and maybe lick his lips, it will help him process what has just transpired during the task or lesson. This may take a few seconds or several minutes, depending on the emotional state of the horse and the degree of difficulty that he felt during the session. This horse needs to feel successful to continue learning, so reward him often. When you are giving the horse a break, it is beneficial if you relax in your body and take your attention off him for a few minutes. If you are working the horse on the ground, you can turn your body and eyes away from him while he processes the information. These are great ways to take pressure off the horse.

With the right training and partnership, the low-energy, unconfident horse can excel in activities such as

- Dressage
- Cowboy dressage
- Western dressage

- Western pleasure
- Ranch riding
- Working equitation

Low-Energy, Lazy, Confident Horse

If you have a horse that is confident and lazy by nature, you will need to be a little creative to motivate him to want to participate in any learning sessions. This horse generally learns pretty quickly but gets bored easily. Break down each task into learnable steps, and once he understands the task, don't drill him over and over again. This horse often needs to understand the reason for doing what is asked of him. Once he understands a task, it is good to put it to use by doing something with it. For example, once you teach a horse to side-pass, do something constructive with it, such as opening and closing a gate by horseback or doing a side pass over a log.

A low-energy, confident horse may

- Be friendly
- Move slowly when he is not motivated
- Show little or no interest in activities
- Love to argue
- Buck or kick out when he is pushed too hard
- Get bored easily
- Tend to not want to go forward very much
- Be mildly curious about new things
- Often be motivated with treats
- Hate repetition

Strategies to Help a Low-Energy, Lazy, Confident Horse Excel

Take your time in the beginning of a session and add in some encouraging fun to help this horse want to participate. This can be done on a lead line or while you are riding. Lazy horses like to stop a lot, so you use some psychology by giving the horse what he wants.

Start in an arena or a large open area. Encourage him by having him stop at predetermined spots in many different places. You can have some cones, pedestals, or poles spread out in the arena. Now that there are obstacles in the arena, you can choose different obstacles or corners to stop at. Pick one, and head toward it with your horse at a walk. When you stop at your first spot, rest for about two seconds. Then head to another corner or obstacle. Stop for only a couple of seconds, and then pick another stopping point to go to. A nice soft pet on his neck and a "good boy" are helpful. After another couple of seconds, you can pick a new spot and head toward it before stopping again.

After a few repetitions with these stopping spots, your horse should start to put more energy into getting to his next destination so that he can stop. The horse may even want to go at a faster pace or gait.

Make sure that you feel some sense of enthusiasm in heading toward the next obstacle. If you are mad or frustrated, it won't work. The horse feels and senses your emotional state.

At first, repeat this with several of the same stopping spots so that the horse sees that there is a pattern to it. This will help him get the idea of the exercise. Once he understands and starts putting in more effort, start mixing up the stopping spots. Horses are smart, and once your horse understands the exercise, he may try to take over and stop at an obstacle without your asking him to do so. You want the horse to stay mentally engaged in the game and wonder where you want him to stop next.

Once his energy and motivation have improved, you can add something that you want to do or work on. If you find that he begins to lose motivation, just add a few stopping spots again to help bring up his motivation. It is important to be creative and progressive with confident horses. If you have a big field, you can set up the same scenario and use longer distances between obstacles, trees, or bushes.

Another example of an exercise for motivating a lazy, confident horse is changing speed within a certain gait. This can be done while you are riding or while he is on a lead or lunge line. If you are trotting, for example, try to trot as slowly as possible without the horse changing gait. Have a plan in your mind of how many strides you want to keep the horse at while at that speed. Let's say that you picked seven strides. After you ride seven strides at a slow trot, ask your horse for seven strides at a fast trot. Now repeat seven slow trots and seven fast trots, and continue with this task until your horse becomes physically and mentally involved in the task and his energy improves. You will probably find your horse starting to have fun with this. Once his motivation has improved, move on to do something different. Horses are pattern animals, and they look for patterns. Patterns help them to make sense of different tasks.

I always like to find ways for my horse to have fun so that he will want to engage mentally in a task. It is fun for me too. Stay on the path of learning so that you can be a great leader for your horse. When you repeat this game in a later session with your horse, it is a good idea to pick a new set of strides to work with. Maybe try ten slow strides and ten fast strides. You can do this at any gait: walk, trot, or canter. You can also choose to practice changing gaits with the same goal in mind. You can choose walk–trot transitions, trot–canter transitions, or walk–canter transitions. Pick how many strides you want to do in each gait, and keep doing it until you see the horse's motivation pick up. Have fun with this game. It will keep him thinking and more mentally and physically engaged with you. This will also help you to be more present in the moment and mentally engaged with your horse.

With the right training and partnership, the low-energy, confident horse can excel at activities such as

- Barrel racing
- Roping
- Ranch riding
- Trail riding
- Mounted police work
- Therapy
- Working equitation
- Obstacle course challenges

As you can see, horses can vary greatly in their innate personal characteristics. It is also important to be aware of the fact that your horse will not always fit perfectly into one of these categories. You may find that your horse shows characteristics in more than one of these areas.

You may also find that your horse acts like a completely different animal when he is in a new environment or when he is in a learning situation. Maybe you have a naturally confident horse that is now acting unconfident in a new environment. If this happens, you will need to adjust your strategies to help your horse gain confidence. If you have a horse that is normally confident but has lost confidence in a certain situation, just help him gain his confidence back. Practice strategies that you would use on an unconfident horse. Once your horse is acting confidently again, you can go back to the strategies that help a confident horse.

When we can find ways to engage a horse's mind and emotions in a positive way, he will want to participate in our activities, and that's where the real fun begins. Understanding these personality traits and having strategies for how to work with them will help you build the partnership of your dreams with your horse. He will appreciate your leadership and respond appropriately.

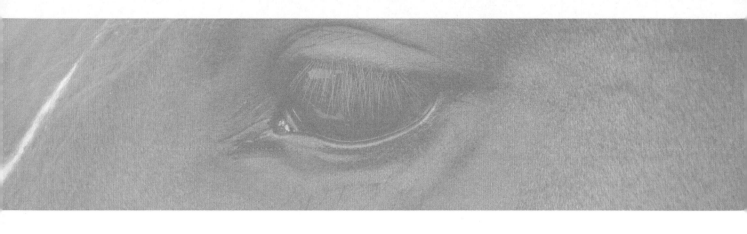

CHAPTER 3
The Horse's Photographic
Memory and Vision

The Horse's Photographic Memory

The horse is a visual animal. Each horse makes mental images of his surroundings, and these images are imprinted into his mind like pictures. Every detail from the broken tree branch to the placement of trash cans in the yard is etched into the horse's mind, as are jumps in the arena. In this way, he is very perceptive to any changes in his environment. Even subtle changes can alert the horse to possible danger. Once something has changed or been moved or added to a familiar area, the horse may become concerned, worried, or fearful.

Have you ever seen a horse get worried when obstacles in an arena have been switched around? Have you been on a trail ride through a familiar area and been passing by someone's property when, all of a sudden, your horse has been spooked and you could not figure out why? It looked the same to you, and you didn't see anything different or scary. Well, your horse noticed that there was a new swing set in the yard or that the trash cans were knocked over. The horse knew that the current environment did not match the picture he had stored in his memory.

It is our job to help our horses gain confidence and learn to be a little braver. We should not get mad at horses for following their survival instincts. Mother Nature tells the horse to run for his life; there could be a mountain lion hiding behind those knocked-over trash cans! For thousands of years, the very survival of horses has depended on their noticing changes in their environment. They have a wide field of vision designed to notice any changes or movement in their surroundings. Horses often react first and think later because time is of the essence when a horse is being stalked by a predator. It may turn out to be a false alarm, but the horse is not going to reason first and react later. The horse's defense system gives him the ability to quickly run away from possible danger and, therefore, ensure his survival.

Understanding that the horse is just doing what Mother Nature designed him to do is the first step in being able to help him gain confidence. If we learn to handle each situation with confidence and fairness, the horse will become braver and start to look to us for guidance when he becomes worried. When you successfully help a horse through a worrisome situation, his confidence in your leadership grows. On the other hand, if you tend to get mad or frustrated when the horse spooks at something, he not only becomes worried about the spooky object but now also feels afraid of you. It is also a problem if you tend to become worried because he absolutely senses your fear and feels that his emotions are validated. If the horse looks at an object of concern and you look at it as well, he thinks that you are concerned too. The best thing to do is to not look around to see what is spooking the horse but instead keep your focus on the path ahead or on the task you are performing with your horse because this helps him focus on you and to use the thinking part of his brain.

Here are some ways for you to tell that your horse is being reactive and responding out of fear:

Facial Expressions

- His head is high.
- His ears flicker around in different directions or are locked onto an object.
- His eyes are wide and unblinking, and the whites may be visible.
- His nostrils are flared.
- He's snorting or blowing loudly.

Body Expressions

- His gait is irregular and lacks rhythm.
- His muscles are tight.
- He is kicking out or bucking.
- He is rearing up.
- His tail is high.

- He can't stand still, bolts, or runs off.
- He jumps in place or to the side and then freezes for a moment.
- He freezes in place and then does not want to move.

Some horses tend to freeze, and some tend to bolt. The reaction depends on the horse's personality. You may see only a couple of these signs, or you may see many of them. If you know what signs to look for, you can better assess what steps of action you can take to help your horse overcome his fear.

For example, let's say that you are riding down a trail, and there is a bundle of helium balloons that has recently dropped to the ground. Your horse becomes worried, and you need to help him become calmer and braver. To start, keep the horse facing the balloons, but back him away from them until he begins to relax. You can tell he is feeling a little better when he becomes more manageable and the expressions outlined previously are a little less intense. At this point, you can zigzag your way slowly closer to the balloons. When you turn to do your zigzag from left to right, make sure that you keep your horse facing the balloons so that he can see them from at least one eye.

If the horse is feeling more confident, you may choose to walk past the balloons and then turn around and pass them in the opposite direction. The horse needs to see them from both directions and from both eyes. The horse's visual image of his surroundings looks different when he is going in the opposite direction. You may even find that your horse has a different reaction to the balloons from the opposite direction. This is because his visual picture looks different when he is facing the opposite way. The horse has very different reasoning power than we do.

When you are riding toward something of concern such as balloons, just keep your eyes looking where you are headed and not on the concerning object. Once the horse feels more relaxed, you can walk past it. Take your time, and he will let you know when he feels better. For less confident horses, it might take longer. Just be patient, and take the time that your horse needs. You do not need to have him touch or smell the object; just help him to lose his fear of it. If your horse needs to move his feet, just help him by directing where his feet should go. You can go sideways or backward or zigzag back and forth. If the horse is reluctant to move his feet, you can try to move just his hind end or front end from side to side until he decides he can move again. Every horse is different, and you have to find what strategy works best for each one.

Another option may be to back away and keep backing up until the horse shows some sign of improvement. Then reapproach the object of fear just a little bit at a time. Keep repeating backing up and reapproaching it until your horse can get a little closer and be less worried. Make sure you keep positive thoughts and emotions in your mind and body as well as a strong confident focus on where you are heading. The goal is to gain your horse's confidence. It also helps him if you can rub him on the neck or withers when he is trying. This may help him relax and you as well. Horses feel better about a petting motion than a pat on the neck. Remember, when they were foals, their mother licked and nuzzled them; there was no patting.

If at any time you feel that your horse is not manageable and you don't have enough skills or confidence to handle the situation, you can back away or dismount. If you choose to back away, have the horse face the object of fear until you feel that he is more relaxed. Then you can turn away from the object and leave the area. If you choose to dismount, first, bend the horse's head to one side so that he can't run off. You can always work on building your horse's confidence at another time when you and your horse are up for the challenge. If at any time you feel unsafe or worried, please dismount from your horse. It is not a failure to get off your horse and handle the situation from the ground. By getting off and not getting hurt, you can actually preserve your confidence and the horse's confidence in you. You may decide to calmly help your horse become confident about the situation from the ground, or you may decide to leave the situation and seek additional help. Whichever one you decide to do, it is OK. Stay safe, and seek out help from a reputable natural horseperson if you need it. I have dismounted many times during uncertain situations, and I will do it again if I feel the need to do so. It is a good idea to have a halter and lead line with you or a bosal and lead line so that if you ever need to dismount from your horse, you are properly prepared. It is always a good idea to practice your emergency dismounts when it is not an emergency. The emergency dismount is discussed in Chapter 20. Always be prepared and be safe.

Another approach that works well for dealing with new, scary objects is to ride with a friend who has a horse that is more confident and just follow the confident horse. Remember that horses pick up on other horses' emotions and your emotions. Horses are often less worried if another horse is confident enough to approach something scary or pass by it. If you happen to have a person with you that is willing and able to lend a helping hand, it would be great to have that person slowly pick up the object of fear—in this example, balloons—and walk away from your horse so that he has an opportunity to follow the balloons. Scary objects become much less scary when they are moving away from a horse. His fear will start to subside, and curiosity will step in and encourage him to follow the balloons. If it is windy and the balloons are making noise and moving around a lot, your horse's fear may be intensified. Don't take on more than you think you and your horse can handle. It is always OK to leave a situation if you are not ready for the challenge. At your home or stables, introduce your horse to new stimuli in a controlled setting. Be creative and look for new opportunities to build your horse's confidence.

Here are some signs that your horse is letting go of his worry or fear:

- He lowers his head.
- His eyes blink, roll back in the head momentarily, or look sleepy.

- He sneezes or rubs his nose on a front leg.
- His breathing is relaxed and regular.
- He is yawning or licking his lips.
- He shakes his neck or his whole body.
- There is rhythm in his movement.
- He wants to roll around on the ground.

All these are good signs that your horse is coming off adrenaline and is relaxing. If you are riding and he is not on a lead line, rolling on the ground can wait. Just know that when you take his saddle off, there is a good chance that your horse will be ready to roll in the dirt. If you have some soft dirt or sand you can take the horse to, it would be a special treat for him. Giving your horse a nice soft place to roll after a ride is always a good idea. It helps him to relax, let go of tension, and readjust anything that may be out of alignment in his body. When the horse lies down and rolls while you are present, it is a sign that he trusts you, and this can be a building block to a better relationship.

The Horse's Vision

Because the horse's eyes are on the sides of his head, he has a wide range of view with only two blind spots. One blind spot is directly in front of his head, and the other is directly behind his tail. Horses can also use their eyes independently or together. Observing the horse's ear movement will let you know what his eyes are focusing on and where his attention is. If both ears are focused in the same direction, his attention is on one specific object or area. For example, if both ears are pointed forward, the horse is focused on something in front of him. If the ears are moving independently in different directions, the horse is using his eyes independently and is focused on two different objects or areas at the same time. For example, if you are working your horse in a round pen and he has the inside ear on you and the outside ear is flickering around, the horse is paying attention to you and the area outside the round pen at the same time. On the other hand, if his inside ear is on you and the outside ear is positioned in the same way, the horse has all his attention on you.

Walking around the Blind Spots of a Horse

If you stand directly behind your horse and he did not see or hear you approach, he can easily spook, buck, or kick out when he realizes that someone or something is there. If you are walking from the side of your horse to the back of your horse where he can't see you, it is a good idea to have a hand on him as you go so he feels you making your way to his hind end. Stay safe, and always make sure your horse is aware of your presence. When you are directly in front of your horse, keep in mind that you are in his blind spot, and he can't see if you are asking something of him. It is a good idea to get in the habit of approaching your horse from the side instead of directly from the front.

Vision during Jumping

It is good to be aware that when you ask a horse to jump an obstacle, he will be executing the jump blindly. He will need to raise his head and use his binocular vision to see the jump from a distance, but as he gets closer, it enters the blind spot at the front of his head. So, the horse needs to trust you in order to be willing to perform the jump. If you are teaching your horse to jump, give him time to build confidence that he can do it. If you push him and force him to execute the jump, he will not learn to trust you. If he hesitates to make a jump or stops and is worried, give him a moment to assess the jump without any pressure from you. Let him smell it and paw at it if he shows a desire to do that. Let his emotions calm down, and then you can ask him to back away several feet while he is still facing the jump. When his head comes down and his breathing relaxes, you can ask him to go forward again. Keep advancing and backing away as many times as the horse needs to so that he can begin to think his way to being able to execute the jump. If you are pushing him while his emotions are up, he will not be able think clearly and will just become more emotional. You have to give him time. Another great strategy is to have the horse walk a short distance away from the jump. When you see his head lower and feel some relaxation in him, you can turn around and approach the jump again. Do this as many times as you need to in order to build his confidence so that he can trust your judgment and jump the obstacle. If the jump is too high, maybe start with a shorter jump. It is not a failure to start with a smaller jump. This sets the horse up to be successful one step at a time. When the horse can make a small jump with his head low and his body relaxed, you will be ready to increase the height of the jump. When he does get brave enough to perform the jump, give the horse a short break, pet him, and reward him for it. Let the horse think about it for a few minutes so he can process the information. Taking the pressure off him includes relaxing your body and facial muscles, turning your body away from him if you are on the ground, and taking the pressure off the reins or lead line. Let the horse know that he has done well. If you give him time to sigh, blink, and lick his lips, his emotions will come down, and he will try harder next time. Then it will be time to do something different for a while so that the horse does not feel drilled but feels successful instead.

Arena Riding and Visualization out of Both Eyes

At the beginning of your ride in an arena, it is a good idea to ride your horse around the arena to the left and to the right. The horse needs to see his environment from both directions. This way, he will get a clear picture of the arena from both eyes. Knowing what his surroundings look like can help him to feel more relaxed and confident and make it easier for him to focus on you. Even in a familiar arena, there may be something different within the surroundings that the horse notices, so let him see everything from both directions every time if possible.

The Horse's Depth Perception

Horses have very poor depth perception. You may come across a puddle, stream bed, pond, or lake and find that your horse wants nothing to do with it. It may be a puddle that is only a few inches deep, and your horse may stop, snort at it, and refuse to cross it. You may be wondering why he is making such a fuss over just a little bit of water, but he does not know how deep it is. Even when you're approaching a deep or large body of water, some of the same types of strategies discussed in the next section can be used. I suggest that if the body of water you are trying to cross has a narrow part, start in that area first and build your horse's confidence. If that is not possible, that's OK; it would just make the process a little easier for your horse and for you.

Strategies to Help Your Horse Gain Confidence with Water or Water Crossing

Helping to build the horse's confidence with water crossing can be accomplished on a lead line or while you are riding; it just depends on your comfort level and abilities. When your horse reaches the limit on how close he believes he can get to the water, you can confidently express to him that he is OK by staying calm and rubbing him on the neck. If your horse wants to smell the water or paw at it, that is OK. Give him time to explore the water. When he stops exploring the water, you can back away from the water a little ways and then try to reapproach it. Take note of how close he was to the water before you retreated. If you can see the hoofprints that your horse left the first time he approached the water, that will be a big help. As you reapproach the water, look straight ahead to where you want the horse to go, maintain calm, confident energy in your body, and head for the water. If you have a riding crop, a lunge whip, or a stick and string, you can add a little rhythmic tap–tap motion on the horse's shoulder or behind the rib cage if you are riding or tap the ground behind the horse if you are on the ground to encourage forward motion. Once your horse is moving forward, it is important to take the pressure off him by letting some slack into the lead rope or reins and stopping the motion of your stick or riding crop. The horse needs all the pressure stopped so that he can think his way through the challenge. Your goal is to get him just a little closer to the water than he did the first time. Maybe you will get only an inch or two closer to the water, but it is still progress. Retreating from the water momentarily after the horse has put in some effort helps build his confidence. He needs to know that you are not going to push him too far past his comfort level. It is also a good idea to reward his efforts with a "good boy" or "good girl" and a pet on the neck. The quicker you can take all the pressure off the horse when he is trying to put in an effort, the quicker he will learn and put in more effort. Repeat this as many times as it takes. Don't be in a hurry. You are there to help him gain confidence and learn that he can overcome his fears. Keep this in mind and make this the goal instead of getting him into the water, and you will go far.

If the horse does not make it into the water on the first day but you made progress and he got closer, that is OK. It is still progress. If the horse begins backing away on his own, just back up with him, wait for his head to lower and his breathing to relax, and then ask again. Use a light tap–tap motion with a stick or riding crop on the withers, toward the back of the rib cage, or behind the horse to encourage him to take a step forward. When the horse stops or quits trying, you can choose to take a few steps backward as a reward or ask for another step forward. If the horse is too worried, just back away for a moment and then reapproach the water. It is important that you do not put push the horse forward while he is trying to figure it out. When the horse takes a step forward, paws at the ground, or smells the water, stop tapping with the stick as a reward for trying. Remember that you are learning together, and it may take a little more time. The better your skills get, the faster it will happen in the future.

When your horse is smelling the water or pawing at the ground, just relax your body, shoulders, and facial expression and smile. The horse will feel your shift in emotions. This will give him time to figure it out without any additional pressure from you. If you are mad or frustrated, the horse will feel that as a form of pressure. If you are losing your patience, it will benefit both you and your horse if you take a break and try again later. No good can come from a session that is full of negative emotions.

If at any time your horse spooks at the water and tries to leave, it is OK. This is a time to help the horse with his confidence; you need to stay calm and patient. Let the horse back up a few feet or walk away for a moment so his emotions can calm down. Wait for his head to drop below his withers and his breathing to relax. Once you see that the horse's emotions have calmed down, you can bring him back to the water and try again. Remember that the goal is to look for moments of effort from the horse without him getting overly excited. If the horse can calmly think his way into the water, it will be even better next time. The horse may get a little sticky with forward movement from time to time, and you may have to add pressure to motivate him to go forward. That is OK as long as it is done in a fair manner. Seek out moments when you can reward the horse for trying. If you are riding, do not kick him to go forward. Instead, add a gentle squeeze from your calf muscles and back it up with a tap–tap motion from a riding crop or stick on the shoulder or on the back of the rib cage if necessary. As soon as he begins to move forward, take all the pressure off by stopping the tapping and leg pressure, and allow him time to think his way forward.

If the body of water has walking room around the water's edge, it may help the horse to walk parallel to the water for a while to get comfortable just being next to it. When he begins to relax a little, you can slowly get closer and closer to the water as you walk him parallel to it. Work on shortening the gap between the water and your horse until he is ready to touch the water. Let him decide how slow or fast he can advance toward it. The more worried the horse is, the more time you will need to take. If he is beginning to relax, you can advance a little closer to the water. It may be only a foot or two at a time, and that is OK. You can't hurry confidence. Give the horse time to explore, and it will build his confidence.

As with any opportunity to build a horse's confidence on obstacles, sometimes a horse's adrenaline will come up, and he will become worried if you have been too firm or pushed too hard or if he is just less confident by nature. Part of troubleshooting is trying to figure out what the problem actually is. If one strategy does not work, try another. Just make sure the strategy feels good and appropriate to you and is fair to the horse and you are not choosing it out of frustration. There are so many different ways to solve a problem, and every horse is different. Water crossings are more challenging to horses because of their poor depth perception, but building your leadership skills and the horse's confidence applies to all areas of horsemanship.

We need to remember that we are working on the horse's confidence. A body of water, balloons, trash cans, and other challenges are just obstacles to help us teach him how to become more confident. If your horse is becoming agitated and his adrenaline is escalating, there is a good chance that you may have gone too fast, pushed too hard, or become mad or frustrated. This is a good time to retreat, take a break, and troubleshoot. Some horses need more thinking time when they are trying to accomplish a task, and it is up to you to figure out what the horse needs to be successful. This is not about getting the horse into the water at any cost. This is about teaching your horse that he can trust you and overcome his fears with your help and guidance. If it is done correctly, the time will come when he will get in the water and be relaxed about it. We just can't put a time limit on it. We have to let the horse decide how long it is going to take, and every horse is different. If you are learning and your timing and skills are not the best, that will add to the challenge. Remember, it is not a failure to ask for help; your horse will thank you for it, and your relationship will grow.

CHAPTER 4
How Horses Learn

The release of pressure is what teaches the horse. End of chapter. Ha ha ha!

How many times have we all heard that phrase? What does it really mean? What does it look and feel like to us and the horse? When we are teaching our horse a maneuver such as backing up, he knows that whatever he did right before the pressure was taken away was the right thing. As human teachers, we apply just enough pressure to motivate a horse to take action. If we are perceptive to the horse's willingness to try to take the action that we have requested of him, in a perfect word, we would immediately release the pressure. The horse would then know that his action was the correct response.

When we are teaching horses, it is important to use phases of pressure to help motivate them to respond. Remember to be consistent in the manner in which you use the phases of pressure. Start by softly asking your horse to respond to your request, and if he does not respond, you can add a little bit more motivating pressure until he makes a decision to respond. Every horse is different, and the amount of pressure needed will vary from horse to horse. A very sensitive horse will most likely need only a small amount of motivating pressure to encourage a response. A confident, bored, or lazy horse may need a little more pressure to be convinced that he needs to respond. Always start with the lightest pressure possible, and add additional pressure only if it is needed. If you use too much pressure or are too quick and harsh with the amount of pressure that you use, you can scare your horse or make him mad or even confused. On the other hand, if you do not use enough pressure to motivate your horse, you will be ineffective or ignored.

You have to get a feel for your horse and play with different amounts of pressure to see what is effective. If you learn to look at this process as a form of two-way communication and take great care in how you apply the pressure and when you take it away, you can begin to build a wonderful rapport with your horse.

Let's consider a wild mustang herd. In this situation, appropriate amounts of pressure are used every day. If the lead mare decides to take the horses to a watering hole or to a new grazing area and some of the horses do not follow, the stallion will be at the back of the herd, putting pressure on the horses that are not keeping up. This will encourage those horses to follow the lead mare. The stallion will do whatever he has to do to convince these horses to keep up. He might pin his ears back, chase after them, and bite them if necessary. He is letting them know that they will be much more comfortable if they follow the herd. Once they comply, he takes the pressure off and relaxes his body and posture.

As human teachers or leaders, we need to communicate with our horses in a way that makes sense to them. In this way, we have a greater chance of success.

There are many ways to apply pressure. Keep in mind that applying pressure is very different from forcing a horse to respond. Forcing involves negative behaviors and actions from a person such as

- Acting mad
- Acting frustrated
- Yelling
- Whipping the horse
- Kicking the horse to go or to make the horse yield to their leg
- Hitting or smacking the horse
- Jerking on the reins or halter
- Making rigid movements

These are behaviors that a horse does not understand. No one wants to be beaten or forced into submission. There is no rapport here. Horse–human relationships will never flourish until people learn the difference.

Applying positive pressure involves some type of stimulus to encourage a horse to respond to a request. Here are some positive examples you can use to apply pressure to encourage an action from your horse:

- Bring up the energy in your own body by taking a deep breath, standing taller, and smiling.
- Gently add a soft squeeze with your legs to encourage forward motion while you are riding.

- Gently exert light pressure with one or two reins to encourage a horse to go left, right, or backward if he does not respond to your legs or seat.
- Use a gentle, rhythmic tap–tap–tap with a riding crop to encourage forward motion or to move a particular part of the horse's body if the horse does not respond to your body aids.
- Apply phases of pressure (see Chapter 11, "Using Phases of Pressure to Accomplish a Task").
- Use a stick with an attached string or some type of lunge whip to apply pressure behind the horse when he is on a long line to encourage forward motion if necessary.
- Use a verbal clucking or kissing sound to encourage forward movement.

Applying pressure teaches the horse that if he does not respond to your request, things will start to get uncomfortable for him; this is just like the pressure the stallion applies to the herd. However, if your horse responds appropriately, the applied pressure will be taken away. You can also show your horse that you are happy with his efforts by relaxing your body, smiling, looking pleased, and petting him. Treats can be used as long as they are given after a positive response is offered by the horse. The treat should not be shown ahead of time to the horse to coax the horse into responding to you. That would be considered a bribe instead of a reward. Positive emotions and rewards can go a long way with your horse and in your relationship. Next, I discuss some examples of how we can replicate herd behavior.

How to Motivate a Horse to Back Up

While sitting on your horse, take the slack out of the reins very slowly, retain light contact, sit up straight, and tuck your tail bone so you are sitting where your back pockets would be; rhythmically move your legs up and down if necessary. The moment the horse begins to back up, relax your legs, and release the reins when the horse takes a step backward. Add the leg pressure only if he does not start backing up when you shift your weight back. Make sure you are not acting mad or banging your legs on his rib cage. Just lightly touch his ribs with your legs in a rhythmic manner if needed. By doing so, you are letting him know that standing still is no longer comfortable and that he needs to back up. The moment he steps backward, stop, and reward him by taking all the pressure off. Do this by releasing pressure from the reins, relaxing the energy in your body by softening your thoughts and muscles, and relaxing your legs gently by his sides. Once your horse understands your request, you can ask for an extra step backward and slowly keep adding more steps. The same principles apply if you want to work on having him back up more quickly. Look for a little better response than you had previously, and stop and reward him when he puts in more effort. It is best to work only on one specific piece of the task at a time. So, work on speeding up the backup, improving the straightness of the backup, or increasing how many steps he is backing up. Otherwise, the horse will get confused. Improve one element of the task before moving forward with another, and then you can put them all together.

Using Pressure to Maintain a Walk, Trot, Canter, or Backup

Let's say you are working on a trot. You ask for a trot, and your horse trots for a few strides before breaking gait and beginning to walk. You want to let him know that he will be more comfortable trotting, so you add a little pressure to ask him to trot again. The moment he trots, you take the pressure off and just focus on riding along with him. Adding pressure could be done by taking in a slow, deep breath and gently squeezing the horse with your calf muscles. If there is no response, you can add a smooch or clucking sound followed by a light tap–tap with a riding crop if needed. It is important to be consistent and use the same cues in the same order every time so that they will make sense to your horse. Make sure you also have a sufficient amount of energy in your body to show him that both of you are maintaining sufficient energy to keep the trot going. Do not nag him to keep trotting. Just engage in the trot with him. As long as he keeps trotting, you should keep the pressure off so that he knows that you are pleased with him. This means you should not squeeze him with your legs or cluck at him after he has responded appropriately. He will soon learn that if he breaks gait, the pressure will return, and he will become uncomfortable until he is trotting again. Have a plan in your head for how long you would like your horse to maintain the trot. Don't ask for too much when you are teaching him; just ask for a lap or two. Once he has achieved the goal, you can let him stop or slow down to a walk for a short period of time as a reward, and pet him gently on the neck. Relax your body and your breathing, and give the horse a moment to feel good about his accomplishment. This is a big reward for the horse.

When you stop and give your horse a break, watch to see if he is looking sleepy, blinking a lot, yawning, or sneezing. These signs show that he is thinking and processing what happened during the lesson. This is a good time to just sit back and relax for a few minutes. Wait until he begins licking his lips. This is a sign that he has understood something significant in the lesson. If he sneezes, a softer sneeze shows more relaxation. By giving him this time, you will both benefit in the long run. Once he starts looking around and acting more alert and the tired look goes away, you will know he is ready to move on.

If you feel you were successful and gained progress on the task you just completed, you can recheck it on your next session. If you ask your horse to repeat the task the next day and there is noticeable improvement, that is a sign that the previous session was a success. It means that you communicated effectively, and your horse understood. If, on the other hand, your horse shows worry about repeating the task, there was some mix-up in communication, or there was too much pressure, and the horse had trouble thinking his way through the lesson. There is no need to get frustrated or mad if this happens. Consider the situation feedback to let you know there is a problem and you may need to seek out another solution. Just try to troubleshoot and pinpoint where the problem is, and slow down or take more time when you teach or repeat the task. Sometimes, the message is not clear enough for the horse to understand. Remember, your horse is doing his best to comprehend what you are trying to teach him. Sometimes, the timing of the pressure release is not good. He may not understand when he got the right answer, and if this is mixed with frustration from you, he may get confused. Sometimes, the horse is just not sure what was expected of him because there was too much stimulus coming at him; this may be the case if you tend to pull on the reins too often, the bit bumps his mouth a lot, or you let your legs bump him when you are not asking for something. When that happens, a confident horse might start mentally tuning you out, and an unconfident horse may get nervous or worried. So, when you ask for something, the horse may not be tuned in to you, or he may be too nervous to think his way to the answer. We need to learn how to ride with our body rhythmically moving with the horse and with our hands and legs putting pressure on the horse only at appropriate times for communication. Otherwise, the horse just sees it all as noise and chaos, and he can't make any sense of it.

When you are teaching your horse something new, he can learn very fast. You just need to learn how to ask in a way that makes sense to him and add pressure only when necessary. You have to learn how to release that pressure instantly when you get the response you are looking for. It is really that simple. Simple but not easy.

Last, it is important not to put a time limit on your sessions. It is going to take as long as it takes for the horse to understand, and that is that. The clearer and more effective your communication is, the faster the horse will learn. If you have this mentality, you will begin your sessions in a more focused and relaxed manner, and you and your horse will both be in a learning frame of mind. If you have to quit your session by a specific time, just find a positive moment in your session to do so. Always end on a good note. You can pick up where you left off during your next session. Don't get frustrated if you do not achieve all your goals this time. Horsemanship is a journey, so be easy on yourself and your horse.

CHAPTER 5
Is Your Horse in a
Learning Frame of Mind?

To teach a horse to do something new, improve on a task, or do any job well, he needs to be in a learning or working frame of mind. When you get your horse out of the stall or pasture, it is unfair to expect the horse to go right to work or to learn something new. He needs to be mentally warmed up, and his body needs to be physically warmed up. If the horse was in a stall, he may also need a few minutes of free time to kick up his heels, run around, and maybe even roll in the dirt. If you let the horse have a few minutes of freedom in an arena or large turnout area, he will be more likely to focus his attention on you and the job ahead of him when it is time. Plus, it can be a lot of fun just watching your horse have fun and act like a horse. If you turn the horse out in an arena and he does not do anything after a few minutes, go ahead and prepare him for your time together. Usually, younger or higher energy horses need more time to play and burn off excess energy.

Sometimes, horses will be more apt to kick up their heels and express themselves on a long line or lunge line than when they are just turned loose in an arena. Some horses, such as many unconfident horses, feel better on a lunge line because it helps them feel connected to you. This can give them a sense of safety. I believe that the more we take care of our horses' mental and physical needs, the more emotionally adjusted they will be.

After your horse has had a few minutes out of his living space to just be a horse, your next step is to get the horse ready to learn. When you are working on improving a skill or teaching a new task, it is important that the horse first become mentally calm and responsive to your requests.

There are many ways that you can get your horse mentally engaged with you. If you know how to do ground work, you can put your horse on a long line and encourage him to change gaits, change direction, change speed within a gait, mix up the size of circles, stand on a pedestal, maneuver through obstacles, back over logs, do side passes over a log, or go over some jumps, for example. This can help the horse have some fun and burn off some excess energy, but it will also add to his emotional and mental well-being. If your horse is unconfident, be more consistent and provide less variety as well as smaller circles. If your horse is confident, add more variety for mental stimulation. Be creative, and have fun. Look for signs that your horse is engaging with you mentally and physically. When you learn to notice and understand your horse's nonverbal body language and his present state of mind, you can begin to adapt your plans to accommodate his needs.

Lunging a horse around in a mindless circle to warm him up is not good for his mental or emotional well-being. When you ask a horse to mindlessly go in circles in a round pen or on a line for the mere purpose of wearing him out or trying to gain control or as a form of exercise, it teaches him to mentally tune you out and can cause him to not want to engage with you physically and emotionally. Make it fun, and don't overdo it to the point that the horse gets bored.

Some signs that indicate that a horse is not positively connected to you include the following.

Negative Facial Expressions

- The horse's head is high or looking away from you, and his attention is elsewhere. He is ignoring you.
- His ears are pinned back, flat, or flickering around a lot.
- His eyes are wide and unblinking.
- His nose has wrinkles, one or both nostrils are larger than normal, and he is snorting loudly or sneezing in a loud and fast manner.
- He is grinding his teeth and has wrinkles around the mouth or tight lips.

Negative Body Expressions

- The horse leaves you of his own accord.
- He is unresponsive to your requests.
- He is overreactive.

- He is not interested in you or the task at hand.
- He appears nervous.
- His gait is choppy or uneven.
- He does not maintain the gait you put him in.
- He changes direction without being asked.
- His head is turned or arched away from you.
- He is kicking out, bucking, or rearing.
- His tail is swishing back and forth, quickly and tightly.

Some signs that indicate that a horse is positively connected to you include the following.

Positive Facial Expressions

- His head is relatively low.
- His ears are attentive to you.
- He is blinking.
- His nose shows no wrinkles, and both nostrils are normal size. He is sneezing softly.
- He is licking his lips.

Positive Body Expressions

- The rhythm of his gait is smooth and consistent, and he's maintaining speed and direction.
- He is responsive to your requests.
- His tail is soft and flowing.
- His head is arched toward you.

For confident horses, mix up your routine and add some variety to keep him stimulated and enjoying your time together. Try not to have the horse feel as if he is being drilled. If you find that your horse begins to get worried or bothered by too many changes, use fewer changes and more repetition. It is a balancing act. Every horse is different, and the better you can understand your horse and notice when he is confident or losing confidence, the better you can help him to get back into a positive state of mind.

For unconfident horses, you may want to use fewer changes and more repetition with circles or familiar patterns, such as figure eights. Wait for the horse's emotions to calm down, and look for more rhythm in his gait, for his head to lower to or below his withers, and for his attention to be focused on you. Reward any positive changes you see. Do this by giving him a slight break, a soft rub on the neck, or a change to a lower gait, and say, "Good boy," or "Good girl." Make sure your body softens and is relaxed and happy when you reward him. Your horse will pick up on these cues. This lets him know that you are pleased. You need to reward every positive change, even if it is a small one. This will lead to your horse putting in more effort. He knows that he has done the right thing only when there is a release of pressure and good emotions are coming from you. The quicker you can release the pressure when he has put in effort, the quicker he will learn.

Once your horse is responsive to your requests and in a calm state of mind, he is ready to learn. This process may take only a few minutes, or it may take hours. There are many factors involved, such as where your horse is in his development, his personality type, and his spirit level. Other factors include your environment, your state of emotional fitness, your horsemanship knowledge and skills, how well you can understand his state of mind, and how well you can reward his efforts. Your horse needs you to be a confident leader who is observant of his current state of mind. You also need to be willing to do whatever the horse needs to build his confidence.

Don't be too hard on yourself while you are learning. Mistakes will happen. Brush it off, forgive yourself, and move forward. Nobody goes through this process without making a bunch of mistakes. This is how we learn. Use it as feedback so that you can make different choices the next time. Even the best horsemen and horsewomen in the world still make mistakes. It is OK.

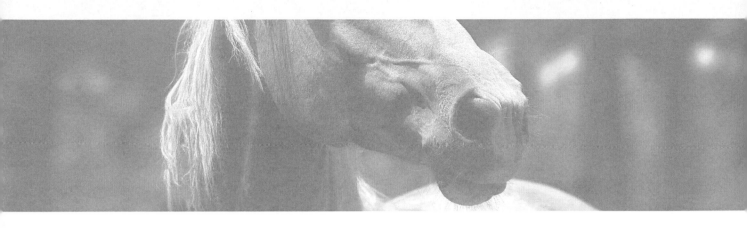

CHAPTER 6
Signs of Tension and Relaxation in Your Horse

Since horses are prey animals, it is natural for them to always be on the alert for signs of potential danger and to be ready to flee at a moment's notice. Horses have very different reasoning power than people do. For instance, a person might see a plastic bag blowing in the wind and be able to use their reasoning abilities to recognize that it is not dangerous. A horse may see a plastic bag blowing in the wind and not be able to understand what it is or whether it is life-threatening. The horse's first reaction will probably be to run away from the plastic bag. When he feels he is far enough away, he will most likely stop and turn around to look at it and see if it is still coming toward him. Then he will make a new decision on whether he is safe or should continue running.

Objects that are new to a horse or objects that are moving toward him will often cause the horse to run first and think later. This is how they survive in the wild.

Horses also become worried when they feel negative emotions coming from another animal or a person. They might not understand what the negative emotion is all about, but it causes them to worry about their own safety. Horses can become worried for a variety of reasons. They will communicate their concerns mostly through nonverbal communication. Some signs of fear are obvious, such as when a horse is scared and running with his tail up in the air, and some signs are subtle, such as when a horse is wrinkling his nose and pinning his ears back. The horse's concern may have something to do with a scary object, a new environment, a windy day, a lack of leadership from you, too much pressure, conflict, or a lack of understanding between you and him.

The key to great communication with your horse is the ability to recognize the fact that he is always giving you feedback. It is up to you to recognize it and understand this communication so you can communicate back to him appropriately. It is also important to note that if there is tension anywhere in the horse's body, there is mental tension in his mind unless the tension is due to pain or injury. There are many signs that may indicate your horse has tension.

Expressive Signs of Tension

Facial Expressions

- The horse's head is high.
- His ears are flickering around a lot, are pinned back or straight back, or are pointed and focused on an object of concern.
- His eyes are wide and unblinking, and the whites may be visible.
- His nostrils are flared, and he is snorting loudly or sneezing loudly and quickly.
- He is whinnying, nipping, or biting.

Body Expressions

- The horse can't stand still, bolts, or runs off.
- He is pawing the ground (this can come from confusion or frustration).
- His tail is swishing quickly or is high and tight.
- He is kicking out or bucking.
- He is rearing up or spooking.
- He has an irregular gait or a lack of rhythm.
- There is tension or tight muscles in his body.
- He freezes in place and then bolts.

Subtle Signs of Tension

Facial Expression

- The horse's eyes are not blinking.

- His ears are tight and stiff. (You may notice this if you gently touch the top of an ear with the palm of your hand and try to gently cup it and slightly bend it. Try this only with horses that are OK with their ears being handled.)
- One nostril is higher than the other, or there are wrinkles in his nose.
- The horse is grinding his teeth, and his lips are tight and tense.

Body Expressions

- The horse's tail is tight. (The tail bone is tight, and the tail bone doesn't move if you try to move it. **Do not attempt to do this if you have a chance of being kicked.** The tight tail is like a hard stick, and the soft tail has flexibility.)
- The horse is frozen in place. (Some horses freeze in place when they are very scared, and it is hard to move them. **Be careful when the horse comes out of a frozen state of mind; he may bolt, rear, or buck.**)

All these signs are the horse's way of expressing the fact that there is a problem. If you ignore the problem, you are ignoring the horse's side of the conversation. As a result, your horse may become frustrated and more fearful, mentally shut down, or display dominant behavior. We are often so busy trying to get something done with the horse that we don't see that the horse is having a problem. You may be doing something as simple as grooming your horse, saddling him, or cleaning his feet and get swished by his tail in your face and think that it was just an accident. It was probably not an accident. The horse is not trying to be mean; he is trying to tell you that there is a problem and you have been ignoring it. The problem may be in your communication with him, or the horse may have something that is physically or emotionally bothering him. Maybe he has a sore or painful spot, or maybe you are being too rough about something. There are many different situations and many different possible answers. Learning to read your horse's nonverbal communication takes time and awareness. Everything your horse does and everything that you do to him and with him mean something to him. Communication is a two-way street, and I would love to help you be able to see the horse's side of the conversation. Once you do, you can start having the partnership that dreams are made of.

When you are riding your horse, you may think it is normal for him to be on adrenaline and a bit excited, especially in group situations or on unfamiliar trail rides. The adrenaline can come from the horse's lack of confidence in a new environment or in you as his leader or from his picking up on the anxiety or frustration from you or other horses and people in the area. The horse is perceptive to all the different emotions that surround him. There are several signs that show your horse is unconfident or worried.

Signs of Tension to Look for while You're Riding

Facial Expressions

- The horse's head is high, and his neck muscles are tight.
- His ears are flickering around a lot or are pointed toward an object of concern.
- His eyes are wide and unblinking.
- His nose has wrinkles, the nostrils are flared, or he is snorting loudly.
- He is whinnying, foaming out of the mouth, or grinding his teeth.

Body Expressions

- The horse is sweating in unusual places, such as the face, under his tail, on his flank area, or on top of his hind end.
- His muscles are tight.
- There is a lack of rhythm in his gait.
- His gait is faster than normal.
- He is frozen in place or does not want to move much.
- With geldings, the sheath of the penis is noisy, with loud air-sucking sounds during trotting.

When you are with your horse, he sees you as part of the herd, so your emotional state and energy level have an impact on his state of mind and energy level. You are his leader, and he counts on you to be calm and confident. If you do not feel that you can be this type of leader for your horse in a specific situation, such as during a group trail ride or a show, it is best to work on building your confidence and skill level up in less stressful situations. Then you can gradually work up to more and more challenging situations. It also helps to ride with likeminded people who also want to set their rides up to be successful. Learn what it takes for you to be the leader that your horse needs you to be. Learn how to read your horse's nonverbal language, and take lessons from a reputable natural horseperson who understands horse language and understands confidence issues in both horses and people. The more you learn and understand your horse, the less need there will be to be fearful. Learn how to know when your horse is mentally and emotionally ready to be ridden. Learn how to get him in a good state of mind so that when you ride, he is ready to be a confident partner. Your confidence comes from knowledge and from knowing how to set up your time together to be successful.

Signs of Calm, Confidence, and Engagement

Facial Expressions

- The horse's head is relatively low with a lack of tension in the neck muscles.
- His ears are attentive and pointed to you.
- He is blinking.
- His nose has no wrinkles, both nostrils are the same size, or he is sneezing softly.
- His breathing is relaxed unless he is working hard.

Body Expressions

- There is rhythm in his gait.
- The horse is responsive to your requests.
- There is a soft sway in his tail.
- There is a no tension anywhere in the horse.

Frustration with horses often comes from a lack of knowledge. It is easy to get frustrated when you don't know how to fix a problem that you are encountering. Once you know how to fix the problem, there will be no need for frustration. When you learn how to fix potential problems and build your horse's confidence, working with him will become fun and rewarding. When you see your horse go from being unconfident or worried to being responsive and mentally engaged with you, it is exhilarating.

Next is a summary of some expressions horses physically display with their different parts and what they can mean. The meaning will vary, depending on a combination of expressions and body posture and on what is transpiring at that particular moment. This may help you to understand what the horse is thinking, feeling, or trying to communicate.

Ears

The horse's ears give you great insight into his thoughts. Ask yourself: What are the ears doing? Are they forward, half back, pinned back, or flickering around?

- If the ears are pointed forward with a relatively low head, your horse is focused where his ears are pointing, and he is probably not worried and may possibly be curious.

- If the horse is looking at you with his ears pointed toward you, he may be curious about what you are doing or what you may want, he may be asking if he can stop working or come closer to you, or he may be asking you a question, such as what you would like him to do. Whatever you are doing at that moment could give you an idea of what type of question he may be asking.
- If his ears are forward with a high head, the horse is probably worried or concerned about whatever his ears are pointed at.
- If his ears are half back, this can mean several different things and depends on what else he is doing and what is going on around him. If the horse is in motion, he may be focused on a task at hand or whatever is happening around him. If the horse is standing still, he may be relaxed, or if he is also looking sleepy, he is probably processing information in his mind about whatever has just transpired. If the ears are tight with tension, the horse might be worried and might not want to move or might move really slowly.
- If his ears are pinned back, it could mean he is mad, irritated, or frustrated.
- If his ears are flickering around, it shows he is worried, scared, or confused.

Eyes

- Take care to pay attention to the horse's eyes because they will help you determine his mental state. What are his eyes doing? Is he blinking, not blinking with wide open eyes, or looking sleepy?
- Blinking usually indicates that the horse is relaxed or thinking and processing information.
- If the horse has wide eyes, his head is high with very little to no blinking, and you can see the whites of his eyes, he may be worried or concerned about something.
- If his eyes look sleepy and his head is low, it often means he is relaxed or processing information from whatever has just transpired.

Nostrils

The nostrils also provide information about the horse's state of mind. What do they look like? Are the nostrils regular in size, are both enlarged, or does one look larger than the other?

- Regular-size nostrils usually mean that the horse is not too concerned about anything.
- If both nostrils are enlarged (this may be accompanied by loud, fast snorts), it can mean that the horse is worried, scared, or concerned about something.

- When one nostril is larger than the other, it can mean that the horse is mad, irritated, or frustrated.

Lips

The horse's lips can also provide subtle hints into his mind-set. What do the lips look like? Are they tight and wrinkled or soft and relaxed? Is the horse trying to bite you?

- Tight and wrinkled lips can mean the horse is angry or frustrated.
- If he is biting, it can mean he is mad, fearful, or feeling dominant.
- Soft, relaxed lips mean that the horse is not worried.

Head

The position of the horse's head can provide a more expressive hint about his mind-set. Is the head high, medium, or low?

- A high head can indicate the horse is concerned, worried, or afraid.
- A medium to low head usually means the horse is not worried.

Tail

The tail can also provide hints about the horse's mind-set. Is the tail relaxed, softly swaying, or swishing fast?

- A relaxed tail with no movement or a soft sway back and forth indicates a relaxed or focused horse.
- A tight tail that is possibly tucked under the hind end shows a scared or nervous horse.
- Fast swishes of the tail usually mean that the horse is mad, irritated, or frustrated.

All this physical feedback from the horse shows you his emotional state. If any of these signs are negative, the horse is telling you there is a problem.

CHAPTER 7
Reactive versus Responsive Horses

Horses are reactive prey animals by nature. They can become reactive for many reasons. A reactive horse is one acting out of fear or confusion, reacting negatively to pressure, or spooking. A responsive horse is one that is using the logical side of his brain and is focused and willing to accommodate your requests. Our job as horsepersons is to understand the difference between a reactive horse and a responsive one. We will cover the reactive horse first and then the responsive horse.

The Reactive Horse

Fear

The horse, being a prey animal, can be fearful of many things. His life may depend on this fear. Some examples of things that can make a horse fearful include

- Changes in the horse's environment, such as being away from home and possibly away from his stablemates
- New objects in his environment or objects that have been moved around to new locations
- Foreign objects that he is not used to seeing, especially if the objects are moving toward him

- A new owner or handler. Every person has their own individual way of communicating with a horse, and he can become confused very easily.
- Predatory behavior or a person acting mad or frustrated or putting too much pressure on the horse
- Windy days. It is hard for a horse to distinguish where danger might be when everything in the environment is moving.
- Loud noises, such as gunshots, car horns, popping balloons, screaming, music bands, and sirens

It is our job to notice when fear is coming up in the horse so that we can address it and help him overcome his fear. It is important that we do not focus on what is bothering the horse because if we do focus on it, the horse thinks that we are concerned about it as well. We need to understand and not blame the horse for his feelings and do whatever is necessary to help him gain confidence.

If your horse is concerned about something, there are several ways you can handle the situation. I discuss a couple of options that I have found helpful, but there are many variables, and these depend on what the horse is worried about, your horsemanship skill level, and the severity of his concern.

One option to use when the horse is mildly concerned about something is to continue with whatever you were working on and do your best to continue the task until the horse refocuses on you and the task at hand. If you were not currently working on a task, you can put the horse to work by doing small circles, making changes in direction, backing away from something scary, or side passing. Keep working on the task until you see the horse begin to calm down.

Sometimes, you may find that the horse gets more worried and that his fear is escalating. If this happens, another option is to try working a little further away from whatever is concerning the horse and see if that helps him bring his emotions down and focus on you. Once the horse's emotions have calmed down, you can either retreat from the area or advance closer to whatever was bothering him and see if he feels more confident, curious, and relaxed.

If the object of concern is moveable, one option is to have someone slowly move the object away from the horse until he calms down and potentially decides to get closer and investigate the object. Let the horse decide how close he wants to get to the object, and don't push him. If it is the horse's idea to approach the object, he will gain confidence in himself and his ability to overcome scary situations. At any time after the horse has become curious about the object, you can make a decision to pass it or walk away from it and leave the area with your horse in a calm state of mind. There are more specific examples in other chapters in this book on helping a horse gain confidence with obstacles and situations that the horse finds fearful.

The goal is to help the horse work through his fears and gain confidence in himself and in you as his leader. If you do not have the skills to help your horse calm down, it is best to retreat from whatever is bothering him and seek help from a professional natural horseperson that knows how to build confidence in a horse. Do try to keep the horse facing the scary object by backing away from it until he begins to calm down before leaving the area. If you happen to be riding when the horse becomes worried and you don't feel confident to handle the situation, please dismount and retreat from the situation in the same manner. It can be a great help to have a halter and lead rope on your horse to help in situations like this.

Confusion

Sometimes, the horse does not know what is expected of him and becomes confused. It can be difficult to communicate with and be understood by a horse when we are communicating in a different language. Sometimes, we blame the horse and think that he is just being bad, stubborn, or resistant when, oftentimes, he just does not understand what is expected of him. We think that we are being clear with our request, but from the horse's point of view, we are being confusing. We try to guide and direct the horse, but what he may be seeing is our hands moving around a lot, our legs moving or kicking, our tools swinging and tapping, and our emotions raging, and he can't make sense of it all. Sometimes, we lack the knowledge to understand how the horse perceives us and what he needs to learn and understand to become confident. If we don't add pressure at appropriate times, subsequently release pressure at other appropriate times, and keep all our other aids and body parts quiet, the horse has no way of knowing when he is responding correctly.

When things are not going as planned and your horse is not responding in the way you want, the best thing to do is ask yourself what you can do to better help him better understand. This is one of the lessons that took me a long time to grasp. It was so much easier to blame the horse than it was to accept that I may have been the one confusing the horse.

As you are learning and gaining knowledge, the answer usually lies in trying something different and seeking more information. If you have tried something several times and no progress is being made, you should try something different. Don't practice the wrong thing for too long because you will just be reinforcing the negative behavior or incorrect response.

Negative Reaction to Pressure

Horses are born with a natural instinct to oppose pressure. When we are working with a horse and the horse resists pressure, we often think he is being stubborn or willful. In the horse's mind, he is just listening to his innate instincts. This can be seen in many situations where there is more than one horse occupying an environment. When horses have a dispute over who is more dominant in a herd situation, they will put pressure on each other and resist pressure coming at them from other horses. The horses involved will try to push into each other with indirect pressure, such as pinning their ears, swishing their tails, and pushing their shoulders into the personal space of the other horse. A horse may continue to escalate this pressure by rearing up, backing into the other horse's personal space, or turning his butt toward the other horse to try to get the other horse to back away from the pressure. If the indirect pressure does not work, he will apply direct pressure by biting, striking, and kicking the other horse. The moment one horse backs away from pressure, he is rendered more submissive.

Horses play these same games with people as well. The horse will try to resist any pressure that is put on him so that he can be more dominant. When we get a horse to move away from pressure or back away from it, we are seen as more dominant. This should always be done in a fair manner, one that starts with light pressure and adds additional pressure only if needed, just as horses do with one another.

Spooking

Spooking often happens when a horse sees or hears something that he perceives as potentially dangerous. We may not see what spooked the horse. On the other hand, we may see that it was just something as simple as a rolling tumbleweed and think to ourselves that it is crazy for the horse to be fearful of that. The horse is designed to react first and think later. A horse does not have the same reasoning power that a person has, and he needs to be convinced that the perceived danger is not dangerous after all. Being perceptive to anything out of the ordinary has helped horses survive for millions of years.

If a horse lives in an area where there are lots of tumbleweeds, it won't take long before he becomes accustomed to seeing them moving around and his fear subsides. This is really the big key in teaching horses to be confident. Exposing horses to many different objects, noises, and environments will help teach them to become confident. Be creative, and look for stimuli to expose your horse to. There are appropriate strategies for teaching this to horses, and some of the strategies are discussed in Chapter 13, "How to Help Your Horse Become More Confident," and in several other chapters throughout this book.

A Learned Response to Resisting Pressure

Horses can learn to resist pressure from a repetitive pattern when they display a negative reaction to some type of stimulus and inadvertently have pressure released. This can happen quite frequently by accident. Sometimes, it happens when a person has tried to accomplish a task with a horse several times, and because of the difficulty, the person releases the pressure while the horse is resisting.

An example of a learned response to resisting pressure might be seen while the horse is being backed up. During this activity, perhaps the horse feels pressure from the bit and raises his head high to try to get away from the pressure, and at that moment, the reins become loose. The horse perceives this as arelease of pressure. If this happens several times, the horse thinks that raising his head is the right thing to do because he ultimately gets what he needs with the release of pressure. This is when it becomes a learned response.

At this point, it is a good idea to do some troubleshooting to find out why the horse was originally having the problem. There may be too much pressure on the reins, a harsh bit, or teeth problems, or he may have just been confused. If the problem is the rider pulling too hard on the reins, great care needs to be taken to learn how to maintain a soft, consistent feel on the reins.

Another common learned response of opposing pressure occurs when a horse takes action to bolt or run off when something startles him, and a release of pressure happens when the lead line gets pulled out of the person's hands. If this happens several times and he gets away each time, he begins to pull back as a reflex to fearful moments. The horse may do this while tied or anytime he feels the need to escape. If there is a hitching rail that you can take your horse to so he can learn to stay tied again, try to not tie him, but instead wrap the lead line around the hitching post three to four times, leaving the end of the line loose. This way, if the horse feels the need to pull back, he can go back only a little at a time. Since he can move and is not tied hard, he will feel a little relief when he can back up several feet. The horse can then stop and lean slightly forward, and the tension will come off the lead line. I would do this with a lead line that is at least fifteen feet long. This way, the horse can back up several feet if he needs to with the rope still wrapped around the hitching post.

Physical Signs That Indicate Your Horse Is Fearful

Facial Expressions

- The horse's head is high.
- His ears are flickering around a lot or are locked on an object.
- His eyes are wide and unblinking, and the whites may be visible.
- His nostrils are flared, and he is making loud snorts.
- He is whinnying.

Body Expressions

- The horse can't stand still, bolts, or runs off.
- He has an irregular gait and a lack of rhythm in his movement.

- His muscles are tight.
- He is spooking, rearing up, bucking, or kicking.
- His tail is high or swishing quickly.
- He jumps in place and then freezes.
- He freezes in place.

Positively Responding or Giving In to Pressure

Even though horses instinctually resist pressure, we can retrain them to give in to pressure in a calm and confident manner instead of resisting pressure or overreacting when asked to comply. You can do this by asking your horse to respond to a request and addressing any resistance, worry, or fear. If the resistance is out of worry or fear, you should calmly and methodically repeat the task until the horse can respond confidently without worry or fear. If the resistance from the horse is due to confusion, you need to slow down and figure out what you can do to add clarity so that he can find the solution and respond correctly. If the horse is not positively responding because he is dominant, you have to work on your leadership role, be creative, and find a way to get the horse positively engaging with you. The moment the horse does respond correctly and without worry, confusion, or fear, you need to take all the pressure off him to reward him for his effort. This has to be repeated many times over many sessions until it becomes an automatic response for the horse to respond in this new, positive way. Just because your horse has learned to positively give in to pressure in one situation does not mean that he will now respond appropriately in all situations.

Example: Reactive versus Responsive in Jumping a Small Obstacle

If the horse resists the jump because he is fearful of the jump or executes the jump quickly in a worried manner, he is reactive, not responsive. If the horse is resistant to perform the jump, retreat a short distance away from the jump, and try the approach again. If the horse still resists the jump, walk away again, and reapproach the jump as many times as he needs to gain enough confidence to go over it. Add pressure only when you start heading toward the jump and not at the jump itself. If you add pressure at the jump, it will probably make his response worse and not better. The horse needs to think his way over the jump, and he can't do that in a calm, responsive manner while he is under pressure. Once the horse goes over the jump, assess his reaction. Did he quickly flee over the jump with a high head and wide eyes and act as if he was scared? If this is the case, calmly repeat the jump as many times as the horse needs to execute it easily with rhythm in his gait and a relaxed head and top line. Once you get a calm jump from a horse, quit as a reward for him. It is always best to start with a short jump and gain the horse's confidence with that jump before you add a jump with more height.

Example: Reactive versus Responsive in Transitioning into a Trot

When you ask your horse to trot, does he do so reactively with a high head and a lack of rhythm in his gait? Or does the horse calmly pick up the trot with a level head and rhythm in his gait? These are the types of questions that you need to ask yourself. The quality of the response makes all the difference. If the quality is not good, ask for the trot again until your horse is positively responsive. You can do this by changing gaits from a walk to a trot and repeating this until the horse can go calmly into the trot. If the problem persists, you may need to assess why the trot is not positive. There can be many reasons for a lack of quality in the trot. You may be applying too much pressure when asking for the trot, such as by kicking the horse instead of gently squeezing him with your calf muscles, or you may not be offering a release of pressure when he has responded positively. You should also consider lameness, an ill-fitting saddle, bumping of the reins, and so on.

The Responsive Horse

A horse that is positively responsive to your requests is focused, attentive, and willing. When fear and confusion are out of the way, the horse trusts your leadership abilities, and when you are communicating clearly, he is more likely to think his way through different situations.

Here are some signs that your horse is being responsive out of respect:

Facial Expressions

- The horse's head is relatively level with or lower than his withers.
- He has one or both ears softly pointed toward you.
- His eyes are soft and blinking.
- His nostrils are soft, both nostrils are the same size, and he is sneezing softly.
- He is licking his lips.

Body Expressions

- The horse is willingly and responsively moving forward or moving away from pressure.
- There is rhythm in his gait, and he is maintaining it.
- His tail is soft and flowing.
- There is no tension in his muscles.

For a horse to respond in a positive manner, a request needs to be clear and understood by the horse. Any aids need to be used in a fair manner, and any pressure that is put on the horse needs to be released when he responds appropriately. If the pressure release is done properly and the horse has enough time to think his way to the right answer, it will mean a lot to him, and he will be more likely to respond the same way again.

Example: Responsive Cantering from the Horse and How to Use Phases of Pressure to Encourage a Positive Response

Let's say that you are riding, and you would like your horse to go from a trot into a canter. As you are trotting, you begin by bringing some energy up into your body; this is kind of like building up enough energy to run on your own two feet. You can start by taking in a happy, deep breath, looking forward into the horizon, and starting a cantering motion in your own body. If your horse does not respond, keep your energy up, keep the cantering motion going, and add a light squeeze with your calf muscles. If he still does not respond, keep all these aids in place, and add some light rhythmic tapping motions from a riding crop on his shoulder or behind the rib cage. The moment he begins to canter, take off all pressure, canter along with him, and remember to smile. This will let him know you are pleased.

If, at any time, he breaks gait, just begin the process again in the same manner. Do not try to stop him from breaking gait. Let him make the mistake, and then ask again. This way, he learns that if he breaks gait, the pressure will return, but if he maintains his canter, you will be happy and light.

Maintain your patience, and remember that you are the teacher and the horse is the student. If you are consistent, don't get mad or frustrated, are pleased with his every effort, and don't put pressure on too quickly, he will begin to understand the lesson and become lighter and more responsive.

Don't ask for too many laps at the canter at first; otherwise, the horse will get tired and lose his enthusiasm. It is also a great idea to do several transitions between the trot and the canter to give the horse some motivation. Pick a number such as seven; then trot seven strides and canter seven strides and repeat. Once the horse has more forward energy, you can canter for longer. If you stop cantering before the horse begins to get sluggish, it will pay off in terms of his attitude and future responses. You always want to end on a positive note, with the horse feeling energetic and happy.

Troubleshooting: Strategies to Encourage a Responsive Canter

Let's discuss some strategies to encourage a responsive canter rather than a reactive one. A reactive horse raises his head and tenses up when he is asked to canter. Some unconfident, sensitive horses will do this until they become more confident. One strategy is to keep asking for the canter until the horse begins to comply, and after a few strides, just come back down to a walk or trot. After a few strides, ask for a canter again, using all the same aids you used before. Repeat these transitions for as long as it takes for your horse to begin to show some sign of relaxation in the canter, and then give the horse a break. Each day, you can work toward getting more relaxation and confidence. Take as much time as the horse needs to gain confidence. It may take a day, or it may take weeks or months. Every situation is unique and needs to be treated as such. If you are looking for a good moment to end your session for the day, look for any sign of improvement and quit then. It is important to stop on a positive note if possible. Always check for problems, such as an ill-fitting saddle, too much pulling on the reins, bumping of the reins from inconsistent handling, lameness, or an unbalanced rider. There are so many variables, and examining all the possibilities is the key to success.

Another strategy is to practice trotting slowly for several strides and then change to trotting quickly for several strides; keep repeating this transition from slow trotting to fast trotting until the horse becomes positively engaged in the task. See how slowly and how quickly you can go at a trot. This task often gets the more confident horse enthusiastic enough to start offering a canter when going into the fast trot.

If your horse becomes more worried with all these transitions, you may need to troubleshoot. There may be too much pressure coming from your aids, a lack of understanding by the horse, or a lack of rhythm from you. The horse may also need more trotting steps at each speed, you may need to make sure that you are releasing pressure after each request, or the horse may need more time to work through it. The more unconfident the horse is, the more time it may take.

Troubleshooting: Dealing with a Horse That Is Reactive Instead of Responsive to Your Requests

You can determine that your horse is being reactive to a request if he pins his ears back, swishes his tail, and refuses to cooperate. The horse might become reactive because of a lack of confidence or too much pressure, or it can be a dominance issue, where the horse feels drilled or forced. If the unconfident horse feels too much pressure, he can have trouble thinking his way to the correct answer. Slow down, start with less pressure, and give him time to think. Be very clear with your request, and reward every effort. Keep your emotions and energy positive, and this will help the horse to put his trust in you as his leader.

Some horses, especially confident ones, don't like to be told what to do or may not see the purpose in whatever their riders wants them to do. This type of horse can become reactive and irritated. He needs to be motivated in a positive way so he can become responsive. He needs to know why he should cooperate.

For example, if you are having trouble getting a confident horse to go forward with a responsive attitude rather than a reactive one, you should put some purpose to his forward motion by giving him some place to go, somewhere tangible that is not too far away. Allow him to stop there for a couple of seconds before moving on to another stopping spot. Start by asking for forward motion, and if you get only a few steps, just pet him and reward him for those steps. After you reward him, ask for forward motion again. Stay focused on your destination by keeping your eyes on the spot and maintaining a strong mental focus and intent to get there. If your horse stops again before you get there, just ask for forward motion again, and be pleased when he moves forward. Once you get to the stopping spot, relax for a couple of seconds, pet the horse, choose another destination, focus your attention on that spot, and head in that direction. Make sure you maintain positive and happy energy in your body instead of anger and frustration. Repeat this process until the horse begins to see the pattern and knows that he is just heading from one stopping spot to another. At this point, you can start picking stopping spots that are further away. Once the horse starts to understand that he is just heading to another spot where he can stop and rest, there is a good chance that he will start responding with more enthusiastic forward motion. Once his motivation is up, you can change the game and do something else. If, at any point, the horse starts to lose motivation, add some more stopping spots.

The more you tune into your horse's needs, the more he will do for you. Whatever you do with him, it needs to be fun for both of you. I know it may sound like a very foreign concept to reward a confident or lazy horse that is not motivated by giving him stopping spots and petting him. I thought so too until I began to understand the psychology behind it. Then I tried it, and it actually worked! If you can get the horse mentally engaged in being a partner, his feet will come along for the ride.

CHAPTER 8
Greeting and Haltering Your Horse

Before greeting and haltering your horse, do you check to see whether you have the horse's permission to approach him and put the halter on? This may be something that has never crossed your mind before. It is common practice to walk up to a horse in his stall or in the pasture and put a halter on him without ever thinking about how the horse feels about it. Everything you do to a horse and with a horse means something. You are either building rapport or destroying it. So, when you approach a horse, do so mindfully. Check to see what his expression looks like and how he feels about your approaching him. Is he happy to see you, or does he ignore you, turn his head away, or walk away? Is the horse comfortable with you putting the halter on him? These are all things for you to seriously consider. How you greet and halter your horse will set up your day's session for success or failure. The horse will give you signs and expressions to let you know whether you have permission to move forward with your session. Forcing your horse without permission will only hurt the relationship you have with him.

Properly approaching your horse is the first step in a successful session. Begin by walking up to him with the halter in hand and watch his expression. Stop and take notice of what the horse's expressions and body language are telling you.

Ears

Start with the horse's ears. What are they doing? Are they facing toward you, half back, pinned back, or flickering around? If the ears are forward with a relatively low head,

63

he is focused wherever his ears are pointing and is probably not worried. If his ears are forward with a high head, the horse is probably concerned about whatever his ears are pointed at. It may or may not be related to your haltering him. If his ears are half back or out to the side, he is likely relaxed. If his ears are pinned back, the horse is tense and mad or unhappy.

Eyes

What are the horse's eyes telling you? Are they blinking, not blinking, wide, or sleepy? Blinking usually indicates that the horse is thinking and processing information. Wide eyes, where you can see the whites, mean that the horse is worried. Sleepy eyes can mean that the horse is relaxed or reflecting on information from whatever has just transpired.

Nostrils

What do the horse's nostrils look like? Are they regular in size, or are both enlarged? Does one look larger than the other? Are there wrinkles around them? Regular-size nostrils usually mean the horse is not too concerned about anything. If both nostrils are enlarged, it can mean that the horse is worried. If one nostril is larger than the other or there are wrinkles around the nostrils, the horse may be mad or irritated.

Lips

Are the horse's lips tight and wrinkled or soft? Is he trying to bite you? Tight and wrinkled lips can indicate anger or frustration. A biting horse may be either mad or fearful. However, soft lips show that the horse is not worried.

Head

Is the horse's head high, medium, or low? A high head can show that the horse is concerned, worried, or afraid. A medium to low head usually means the horse is not worried unless there are other negative signs from expressions listed previously. Does the horse turn his head away from you or toward you? If the horse turns his head away from you while you are approaching or trying to halter him, you do not have permission to do so. If he turns his head toward you with a soft look on his face, you do have that permission.

Body Movement

Does the horse look at you or walk away from you? He may be looking at you out of curiosity or willingness as long as his expressions are soft and positive. If he is walking away from you, he is not interested or is concerned or worried. Is his tail relaxed, softly swaying, or swishing fast? A relaxed tail indicates a relaxed horse. A fast, swishy tail usually indicates a mad or frustrated horse.

These signs that the horse expresses when you first approach to greet him are feedback that let you know what his emotional state is. If any of these signs are negative, he is telling you there is a problem. It is important not to ignore these signs. If you see any negative signs while you are approaching your horse, immediately stop, stand still, relax, exhale, and smile. Often times, this will peak your horse's curiosity because it is not normal predatory behavior. Keep standing still, and see if the horse's negative expression goes away. He may even turn his head to face you and possibly turn his ears towards you. If the expression does not change, try taking several steps backward, away from the horse, and watch for him to become curious about you and this new approach. Once he gives you a positive expression, you have permission to begin to approach him again. If at any time his expression becomes negative again, stop and repeat the same steps. Make sure to maintain positive thoughts and a relaxed body. Take your time, and the horse will let you know when you have permission to be next to him. This process will be different for every horse because every horse has had a different life experience. This may work right away, or it may take time. If you don't seem to be able to make progress, please seek help from a natural horseperson that understands horse behavior. You can also contact me for coaching. If you approach your horse and the signs are positive, you can see if he is willing to greet you by offering your hand for him to smell. Make sure you maintain positive thoughts and are relaxed in your body. Once the horse is comfortable with you, softly pet him on the neck, gently begin to lower his head, and put the halter on him.

Here are some signs that show you may have permission to put the halter on the horse:

- The horse willingly approaches you or allows you to approach him while you both have positive attitudes and positive expressions.
- He willingly stands still while you are putting the halter on him.
- He moves his head toward you as you go to halter him.
- He keeps his head low and has a soft look on his face with no tension in his face, ears, or body.
- He puts his head in the halter.

If, at any point, the horse begins to turn his head away or raises his head up high, slowly, gently, and with a soft feeling follow his head with the halter in your hand without trying to put it on him. Keep your hand a few inches away on the side of his muzzle. Move it at the same speed as the horse moves his head so that you maintain the same few inches of distance. As soon as his head stops, stop moving your hand, and keep your hand those few inches away from his muzzle. When your horse decides to move his head even a tiny bit down or toward you, take your hand and the halter away from his face. Relax, turn your body slightly away from his face, breathe softly, and smile. Try again, and repeat the same process. The horse will start to realize that if he turns toward you, you will take the hand and halter away; this will help him lose his fear of being haltered or trapped. This is a big reward for your horse; it takes all the pressure off him and lets him know that he responded correctly by moving his head toward you. Now, wait a few moments, and look for some of the signs of relaxation. Give the horse this time to think. If you do not get any positive signs within a minute or two, go ahead and try again. There may have been some confusion on the part of the horse if the timing of moving your hand away when he moved his head toward you was not good. He may not have understood what was taking place. You want him to realize that it is more comfortable to lower his head or turn his head toward you than it is to turn away from you. This may take some time. The horse may have had bad experiences, or he may not be used to the fact that his opinion matters. Repeat this task until he shows a positive response and moves his head toward you every time or at least does not show any negative reactions by moving his head away. In this way, he will learn that the positive thing to do is to follow your hand and the halter. You have permission to halter the horse once you approach his nose with the halter without him moving away or showing any of the negative signs mentioned previously.

If you happen to have a horse that has a habit of raising his head up high in avoidance when you try to halter him, you may want to first teach him to lower his head by using a physical cue. You can put your thumb and forefinger at the top of his mane. Put one finger on each side of his mane and slowly add pressure by squeezing the skin together, like you would with a light pinch. Hold the pinch steady until the horse lowers his head. If, at any point during the process of slowly adding the pinch, the horse begins to lower his head, even a tiny bit, release the pressure immediately. It is the release of pressure that teaches the horse that whatever he did just prior was the correct thing to do. Repeat this process until he lowers his head every time and it eventually becomes level with his withers. Pet your horse, and let him know that he is doing well. Keep your emotions positive, and remember that he is a student. Learning happens more quickly when there is understanding and patience.

Do not worry if you don't get the horse's permission to halter him on the first day. Depending on his fear level, bad experiences from his past, and the learning curve you are experiencing, the process may take several lessons. The good news is that if you end a session on a good note and there was some positive progress, the next session should be more positive and take less time.

Be patient with yourself. Learning takes time. Try not to be mad at the horse or yourself. Negative emotions will not solve anything, and if the horse picks up on them, he will want to avoid you even more. Horses don't understand why a person is angry or upset. Those negative emotions only alert their senses to possible danger.

CHAPTER 9
Saddling Your Horse and Recognizing and Solving Saddling Problems

Taking great care in saddling your horse correctly can eliminate many future problems and enhance your relationship with him. You can tell if someone is a good horseperson by the way they saddle their horse. So, let's be very careful to be as tactful as possible. I will explain the process with a Western saddle since they are heavier and harder to lift. The process is the same for Western and English saddles, except Western saddles often have a back cinch.

Start by brushing the dirt and loose hair off the horse before saddling him. Allow the horse to smell the saddle pad to see if he has any concerns. If he does not, gently place it on his back. If he raises his head or looks worried, put it on and take it off in a slow, rhythmic flow as many times as needed for him to begin to relax and lose his worry. Make sure the pad lands gently and smoothly on his back every time.

Check yourself to make sure there is no tension in your body; otherwise, the horse will pick up on this, and he will continue to feel tense himself. Once he shows signs of relaxation, leave the saddle pad on his back. Pull up the front center part of the pad to a couple of inches above his withers to allow room for them when the saddle is put on and cinched up.

If you have not had practice putting the saddle on without the stirrups hitting the horse's side or if you have trouble gently placing the saddle on his back, it may help to practice putting the saddle on top of a fence for practice. You won't cinch up the fence; this is just to help you learn to put a saddle on top of something with ease and great care. It may sound funny, but your horse will appreciate it. The fewer mistakes you make with the horse, the better.

A good way to saddle a horse, or to saddle a fence, is to first learn how to hold a saddle properly. If you are saddling from the right side and facing the back end of the horse, hold your saddle sideways with the cantle in your left hand, the center on the underside of the saddle on your left hip with the horn facing forward, and your right hand on the front of the saddle. In this manner, you can swing the saddle from side to side in a rhythmic motion on your hip before swinging it over the horse or the fence. Right before you swing the saddle up into place, use your hip and knee to help lift it up. Begin by bending your knees and then push up with your hip and your knees to place the saddle on the horse's back. Look several inches above the horse's back or the fence that you are saddling. This will make your aim better. Once you can land the saddle softly on the fence without any banging or the stirrups clanging, you'll know that you are ready to saddle your horse. Gracefully place the saddle on the horse's back, and check to make sure that the saddle pad still has a couple inches of clearance for the withers.

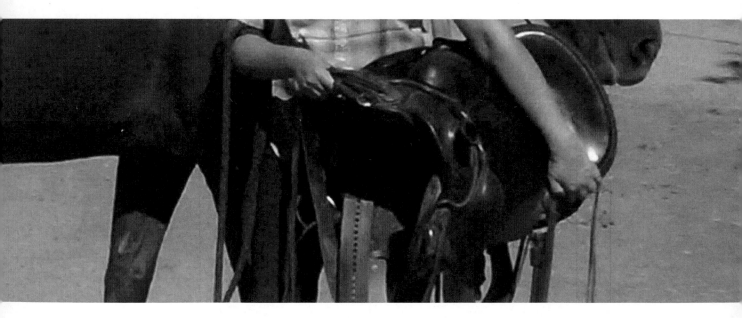

You can cinch up the saddle from either side of the horse, but in this example, we will do it from the left side. When you begin, stand on his left side and have the front of your body facing toward the back of the horse. Gently slide your left hand under his girth, grab the cinch, and gently wrap it around. Petting a horse throughout the process can be beneficial. Always tighten the front cinch first, then the back cinch, and finally, the breast collar, if there is one. After your ride, loosen up the cinches in the opposite order, with the breast collar first, the back cinch second, and the front cinch last. This way, if the horse ever spooks or something goes wrong, there is less of a chance that the saddle will end up underneath him.

It is best if you tighten the cinch in a three-step process. The first tightening should be just enough to keep the saddle in place without it slipping down the horse's side. While you are tightening the cinch with your right hand, have your left hand slightly above the withers, and gently press down on it. This is an area where horses groom one another, and this pressure gives them a feeling of safety and comfort.

After you complete the first tightening of the cinch, it is best to move the horse around a little bit. You can move his front end around and then his back end around, add in some small circles, and back him up a few steps. Make sure the cinch is snug enough that the saddle will not slip underneath the horse if he panics about something. Backing a horse up while moving him around can help him to tap into the thinking side of his brain instead of the reactive side. If the horse is calm at this point, you can cinch up the saddle a little more tightly. Make sure you time the tightening of the cinch with the horse's exhale. Move him around again for a few minutes. As long as he is calm and attentive, you can finish cinching up the saddle one last time. Make sure you complete the process with a smooth, slow motion, and do not use force or quick jerks.

Here are the steps for saddling in order:

1. Place the saddle pad on the horse's back.
2. Gently place the saddle on the horse without the stirrups hitting his sides.
3. Pull up the front part of the pad to make room for the withers.
4. Smoothly tighten the front cinch but not too tightly.
5. Tighten the back cinch and then the breast collar if there is one.
6. Move the horse around, including backing him up, for a couple of minutes.
7. Gently tighten the cinch a little more.
8. Move the horse around again, including backing him up, for a couple of minutes.
9. Finish tightening up the cinch.

When you use this nonforceful way of cinching up the saddle, the horse will feel less of a need to swell his belly and will be less emotional. If he has already had bad experiences with saddling, you may need to do problem solving to restore his trust and confidence. The following signs indicate that the horse may be having trouble with the saddle or the saddling techniques mentioned previously.

Facial Expressions

- The horse's head is high, or he raises his head while being saddled or cinched up.
- His ears are pinned back or tight and tense.
- His eyes are wide and unblinking. Unconfident horses may look sleepy.
- His nose has wrinkles, or one nostril is bigger than the other.
- His mouth is tight, or he is grinding his teeth, nipping, or biting.

Body Expressions

- The horse walks away or will not stand still.
- He is breathing deeply to swell his belly so that you can't cinch him up too tight.
- His tail is swishing back and forth in a fast and tight manner.
- He is kicking out at you.
- He is pawing at the ground.

If you see any of these signs while you are saddling, the horse is communicating to you that there is a problem. Some horses, especially high-energy, young, and dominant ones that live in stalls, may need to move around a little bit before you put the saddle on. It can be very hard for high-energy horses, horses that have been cooped up in a stall, or unconfident horses to be taken straight out of the stall and be cooperative and ready to work. Horses often need a few minutes of freedom of movement to release pent-up energy. Let the horse run around and kick up his heels in an arena, or if you know how, do some groundwork to get the horse mentally engaged with you; it may make a big difference in his willingness to be saddled. The horse may want to roll in the dirt. This is one way that horses let go of pent-up tension. It is also a great way for him to adjust his joints if anything is out of alignment.

Please note that great care should be taken while you are saddling a green horse that is not used to a saddle. The horse may buck or take off and risk having the saddle fall underneath him. There has to be enough knowledge on your part to know the steps that come before saddling and cinching to be successful. The training of a green horse should be done by someone with horsemanship knowledge, experience, and skills. If you have a green horse, please seek out expert help from a reputable natural horseperson. It is better to delay saddling training until you can find appropriate help before the horse has a bad experience and long-lasting or permanent fears are created.

Troubleshooting: Saddling Issues

If your horse is having saddling issues, you should first determine whether the saddle is properly fitted to the horse. Every horse and saddle are different, and an improperly fitting saddle can cause the horse great discomfort. If your horse is showing negative signs during saddling, make sure that the saddle fits properly, has its weight distributed evenly, and is not pinching or blocking the horse's withers from extending backward during motion.

There are clues to help you identify an improperly fitting saddle. When you remove the saddle after a workout, are there any dry spots on the horse's back under the saddle area, especially around the withers? Are there any white spots of hair near the withers? If so, the saddle fit may be creating some harmful pressure points. Clearance around the withers is important for the horse's natural gait and movement. Before saddling, try extending one of the horse's front legs forward by holding it from the underside of the knee with your hand, and watch his shoulder to see just how far back it extends. The area needs to be free to move even with the saddle on. If the bars of the saddle block the shoulders from moving freely, the fit will need to be addressed. Placing the saddle too far forward can also block the withers.

When you take the saddle off after a good workout, check whether the horse's hair is pushed forward around the front area where the saddle fits. If this is the case, the saddle's weight is not being distributed evenly. Ill-fitting saddles have a tendency to push a rider's weight forward. If the rider's weight is too far forward in the saddle, it will make it hard for the horse to lift his front end up and use his hind end correctly. To verify the saddle's position when it is on the horse, place a small cylinder such as a stick of lip balm or something round and a few inches long on the top of the saddle and see where gravity moves it. The saddle is in the proper position if it rolls to the back of the seat. If the cylinder stops in the center or toward the front of the seat, the saddle needs to be elevated in the front.

If you find that the saddle does not fit properly, there are some options to check before investing in a new saddle. Shims may help elevate the saddle slightly off the front end and release pressure over the withers and any other area that may be experiencing discomfort. There are also air gel pads and adjustable air pads that can be used in place of a regular saddle pad. Some of these pads also have pockets for shims. Shims can help, but be careful not to block the withers with them. If the saddle is very narrow in the wither area, these shims and pads may not be enough to correct the problem, but they are worth looking into. You may also need to find someone who is knowledgeable about fitting saddles and shims appropriately. When testing options, remember to keep checking the area under the saddle for dry spots and to look at whether the hair near the front of the saddle is being pushed forward. Ensure that you are not moving the problem to a different area. If the saddle does not fit correctly, the horse will be uncomfortable and have a hard time carrying a rider and doing his job correctly. The horse's comfort is just as important as the rider's.

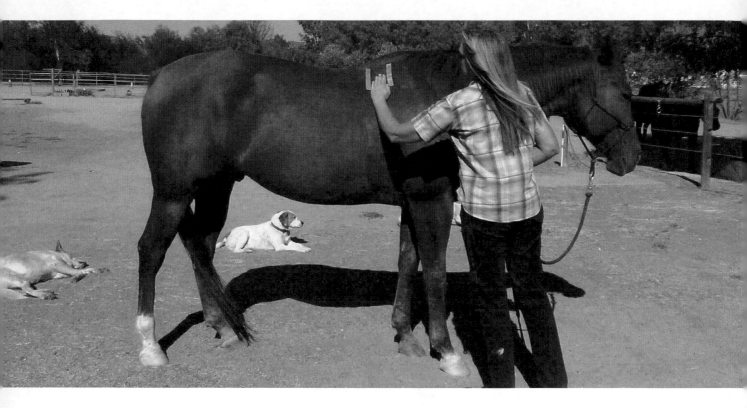

In this photo, the tape on both sides of my hand shows how far the horse's withers extend from when he is standing still to when he is in motion.

Troubleshooting: Cinching Issues

With many horses that have been cinched up too fast or too roughly in the past, you will find that they have trust issues in this area. If you are cinching up a horse and he displays any of the negative expressions mentioned previously, the cinching problem will need to be addressed. There are many possible ways to deal with this issue because every horse and every situation are different. I will explain a few possible solutions that have proven successful for me. If these tips do not work, you may need to seek additional help. There is no single solution; there are only different options, which depend on the horse, his past experiences, and your savvy and knowledge. Whatever you do, don't make the horse feel wrong for expressing his discomfort or fear. He is just communicating with you in the best way he can. If the horse tries to nip at you, place your elbow in such a way that when he turns his head toward you to nip, his jaw runs into your elbow instead. If you smack him, you will just ruin the trust between the two of you. The horse is not being mean if he does nip at you; he is just expressing his concerns. Proper communication between horse and rider is what natural horsemanship is all about.

Possible Solution 1

If you think you may have a cinching problem, try leaving the saddle off and wrapping something around the horse's girth just snugly enough that it does not come off. For example, try tying a lunge rope gently around the girth, and hold the loose end so it does not drag on the ground. You can use any kind of rope that is suitable. Or, if you have a bareback pad, gently cinch that around him. Don't start with the cinch being tight around the horse's girth. Just have it snug enough that it will stay in place. The main focus is getting the horse comfortable with the pressure around his girth area. Let him move around in a round pen or on a lunge line so he can get used to the feeling of having something wrapped around his girth. If you are not causing the horse concern or discomfort, you should see some of the following positive signs in him.

Facial Expressions

- The horse's head is relatively low.
- His ears are attentive to you.
- His eyes are blinking and not wide.
- His nose has no wrinkles, both nostrils are the same size, and he may be sneezing softly.
- He is licking his lips, yawning, and breathing in a relaxed manner.

Body Expressions

- There is a soft sway in the horse's body and tail as he moves.
- There is rhythm in his gait.
- He maintains speed and direction.

Once you see some signs of relaxation, you can let the horse stop and relax, and temporarily loosen the cinch or rope. Letting your horse relax momentarily lets him know he has done well. This will also give him time to reflect on what has just happened. The horse will show this by first looking sleepy for a short period of time and then blinking, licking his lips, and possibly sneezing softly. Give the horse this time to think and process what has just transpired. After you have rewarded him with some reflection time, gently tighten the cinch or rope back up while he exhales, and then ask your horse to move around again.

After you have successfully repeated this several times with positive responses, you can then slowly increase the tightness on the rope or bareback pad and have the horse move around again. Remember that it is very important to repeat this process for as long as it takes to convince the horse that he does not need to be afraid. A horse will often feel claustrophobic when something is put around his girth, and it can take some time to convince the horse that he will be OK, so take your time. It may take weeks, or it may take less time. Pay attention to the signs that he is showing you. If he is tense and high-headed and can't maintain a consistent gait, keep working with him until he relaxes, and then take a break and reward him.

If you find that the horse is worried and not relaxing, just let him move around in a round pen or arena until you see signs of relaxation. Let the horse work his way through his anxiety and realize that he is not trapped. If you add some changes of direction and maybe place some poles on the ground that the horse can jump over, this may help him to keep thinking instead of trying to mentally check out. Going around in circles over and over again is a mindless game, and this will not work to help the horse learn or improve. Add some variety.

With some horses that are unconfident, it may be hard to tell whether they are calm or not because they do not always outwardly express tension in an overt way. This type of horse may look as if he is doing fine, but if you are unsure of his mental state, look at his face and body for subtle signs of tension.

Some of these signs in an unconfident horse may include

- A low head with unblinking eyes
- Tight ears that are stiff to the touch
- Tension on his face, such as wrinkles around the nose or lips
- Irregular breathing
- Lip licking without an open mouth
- Resistance to moving his feet
- A stiff or tucked tail

If you think that the horse is showing these unconfident signs, just give him time until you see signs of relaxation, such as blinking, looking around, soft sighing, and lip licking. When you see some of these signs, loosen the tension around his girth, and give the horse time to stop and think about what has just happened. It is important for you to leave the unconfident horse completely alone by taking all pressure off him while he processes this information. Do this by turning your body and eyes away from him and relaxing until the horse begins to blink, possibly sneeze, and maybe lick his lips. This process could take anywhere from a few moments to several minutes or maybe longer. Don't rush the horse. If you give him the time he needs, he will give you so much more back.

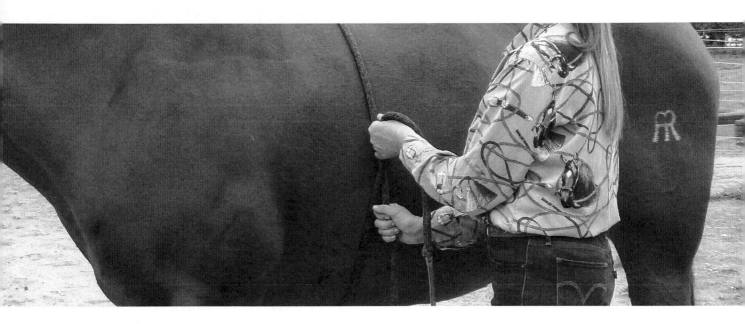

Possible Solution 2

Have your horse stand still next to your side, and take a lead or lunge line, wrap it around his girth area, and take hold of each side of the rope, one in each hand. Very slowly tighten the lines with each hand until you see a slight negative reaction from your horse. Don't do this so fast and hard that the horse has a huge reaction.

Signs of a negative reaction include

- The horse's head getting higher
- His ears being tight, pinned, or flat back
- Wide, unblinking eyes
- Sleepiness, as if the horse is in a trance or checking out emotionally (more likely with a very unconfident horse)
- A wrinkled nose, one nostril being bigger than the other, or slower than normal breathing
- A tight mouth, grinding teeth, nipping, biting, or popping lips
- The horse's tail swishing back and forth, fast and tight
- The horse kicking out, bucking, or rearing up
- The horse trying to leave or pull away from you

As soon as you see one or more of these signs, stop and hold the ropes in a way that maintains the exact amount of pressure you were holding when his reactions came up. Hold it there until the negative reaction decreases, even a little bit, and then release it immediately.

If the horse's head drops just a little or if he blinks, sneezes, or sighs, release the tension, and reward him for trying to accept the pressure. Repeat this over and over, always watching for the moment his negative reaction starts so you can hold the pressure there. Be sure to time the release of pressure to the decrease in his negative reaction. Be patient, and know that this may take some time to successfully accomplish. It may take a few minutes, hours, or several sessions. If you begin to get frustrated or are running out of time for the session, just end on a good note when there is some kind of progress. If you quit during a negative reaction from the horse, you will have just taught him that his negative response was the correct one. When there is no longer a negative reaction, you can try the saddle and cinch again.

Once you can saddle and cinch the horse up successfully, you can add more stimuli to the saddling process. Stand next to your horse, staying out of the kick zone, and start moving the stirrups around with your hand, or tap on the seat to cause some commotion. Start lightly at first, and just as in the previous exercises, when you see signs of worry, just hold the pressure or stimulus at the same level until you see signs of relaxation, and then immediately stop. If you find that the horse is not relaxing and he begins to get worse, you may have gone too fast and may need to bring the intensity down a bit to help him out. You want to build up the horse's confidence so that he does not get worried about a lot of commotion. Just remember to start with a light pressure or stimulus, slowly build up the intensity, and release it the moment the horse responds in a positive way so that his confidence can grow.

CHAPTER 10
Whoever Controls the Movement of the Herd's Feet Is the Leader

orses naturally have a pecking order. There is the number one horse, the number two horse, the number three horse, and so on. Every horse in the herd knows the rank of every other horse. Nonverbal arguments and dominance games happen regularly between horses. There are various reasons, including disputes over who gets to eat and drink first and attempts to gain a higher position or breeding rights in the herd. When a horse is with a person, he will often treat the person as a herd member and play dominance games with them to attempt to become the alpha in the horse–human relationship. In one dominance game, the horse will try to keep control of his own feet and gain control of the feet of whomever he is with. Depending on his particular personality, the horse may be subtle or very obvious. Every time the horse wins the foot-control dominance game, the horse feels that he is climbing up higher in the pecking order. I like to refer to this as a way that a horse gains an advantage over another horse or a person. The following are some examples of how a horse or you can gain advantage in this way.

Advantages Earned by the Horse while on a Lunge or Lead Line

- The horse moves his feet somewhere without permission.
- The horse gets you to move your feet somewhere.
- The horse gets you to move your feet more than he moves his feet.

Advantages Earned by the Horse while Being Ridden

- The horse moves his feet somewhere without permission and is not directed back to where he was.
- The horse drops to a lower gait without being asked and is allowed to stay there.
- The horse changes directions without being asked.
- The horse stops to graze while you are riding someplace.
- You ask the horse to make any type of transition, and he slowly, lazily responds or does not respond at all.

Advantages Earned by You while You Are Working the Horse on a Lunge or Lead Line

- The horse moves his feet somewhere without permission, so you move him back twice as many steps without moving your own feet at all or by moving them very little.
- The horse does something to try to get you to move your feet, and you stay still and move him back instead.
- You direct the horse somewhere, and you move your feet less than he does.
- The horse tries nipping at you, and you have him back up before he bites you without getting upset.

Advantages Earned by You while You Are Riding

- When you are at a halt, the horse moves forward without permission, and you move him backward twice as many steps as he went forward.
- The horse changes to a lower gait, and you immediately and fairly ask him to return to the higher gait without being mean or getting mad at him.
- The horse changes direction on his own, and you immediately put him back on track and are firm but fair.
- The horse stops to graze without permission, and you immediately ask him to go forward and maybe ask for a higher gait than he was at before.

The dominance games horses play can be very subtle. For a rider to win the games, awareness and timing are critical. The following are a few examples of situations in which you may find yourself engaging with your horse in dominance games.

Example of Earning an Advantage with Ground Manners

Let's say that you have your horse on a lead line, and he is standing close to you as you are talking to a friend. Your horse is standing there patiently for a few minutes and then decides to take a step toward you or toward something he sees on the ground. If you ignore it, your horse feels that he is in charge and has just won an advantage; he has earned a point. Don't be mean or get mad. Just direct him firmly and fairly back to where he was in a calm manner and then add another step backward for each step he took forward. Now the trick is that you have to figure out how to do this without moving your feet or by moving your feet very little. If you move your feet more than he has moved his feet, he gets the advantage.

One strategy you can use to back a horse up is to stand up tall, take a large deep breath, and rhythmically swing some type of stick or lunge whip back and forth horizontally toward his chest, keeping a steady rhythm in the stick until he takes a step backward, and then stop the stick momentarily as a reward. When the horse complies, relax the energy in your body as a reward. You can accomplish this by exhaling and relaxing your jaw, your shoulders, and the rest of your body. Keep enough slack in the lead line or rope so that when the horse takes a step backward, he does not run into the end of the line. That will just confuse him. If he does not respond by backing up, increase the speed of the rhythm with the stick until he does respond and then stop immediately upon compliance as a reward for the horse. Don't go after the horse with the stick; stand your ground, and let the horse move his feet. Start by slowly swinging the stick horizontally, and slowly swing the stick faster if there is no response. The more unconfident the horse is, the more slowly you need to begin. Remember to quit swinging the stick the moment the horse responds. It is also important to understand that if you are mean or get mad at the horse and don't treat it as if it is a game, you lose the advantage, or the horse gets scared and confused, and your rapport is damaged.

Oftentimes, you may be standing there talking to a friend, and your horse will slowly and gradually move into your personal space. He may act as if he is busy smelling something on the ground or as if he is nuzzling or smelling you, and you may try to get more comfortable by moving a step away. It is so subtle that you do not even realize that you have moved because you are engaged in your conversation with your friend. Surprise! Your horse has just gained an advantage by playing his game, and you are completely unaware. Next time, he may be more aggressive about it, and you'll begin to wonder why your horse is being so pushy. You should not get mad at him for this; he is playing a game. That is what horses do. It is your job as a leader to be aware, always be observant, learn, and win these games.

Example of Earning an Advantage while You Are Getting Ready to Ride

You attempt to get on your horse, and he tries to walk away. He does not wait for you to ask him to go; he just starts walking. This is a great example of your horse gaining an advantage and thinking that he is the leader. Have you guessed what you should do yet? Yes, back him up twice as many steps as he moved forward. Then he needs to stand still until you ask him to go forward. When he tries to go forward again, just count the steps that the horse walked forward and then back him up twice as many steps. Keep repeating this game as many times as it takes for him to get the idea.

If you are consistent, it should not take too long. Take as much time as the horse needs to understand. If the horse has been walking off like this for a while, it may take some time for him to realize that you are serious and there are new rules to this game. Practice patience, and take the time to be his calm, focused, and patient teacher. If you practice good teaching methods, the following sessions should take only a fraction of the time. Bad habits that a horse has adopted won't go away overnight. This only makes sense because your horse did not adopt these bad habits overnight, but with good teaching skills from his human partner, he will get better day after day.

Example of Earning an Advantage while You Are Riding

Let's imagine that you are riding in a large field that has lots of patches of bushes or trees. You are working on riding different circles around these patches while at a trot. Your horse's job is to follow your directions while maintaining the trot. If, at any time, the horse chooses to turn in a different direction than you have asked for or if he drops to a lower gait, you immediately remind him of his responsibility by putting him back on course at a trot. This is a great game to keep the horse focused on you and to help him learn what his responsibilities are. He is to maintain his gait and direction until further notice. It is important to stay focused on the goal and have patience. It is also very important that you don't micromanage the horse by pulling on his reins and kicking him or holding constant pressure on his reins. Ask lightly with leg pressure and/or light rein pressure, and release the pressure or lighten it up when the horse is trying. When you notice the horse improving on this task, reward him. You can reward him by releasing the pressure, petting him and telling him how good he is, changing to a lower gait, or stopping for a few minutes as a big reward. Show your enthusiasm for his efforts, and he will begin to try harder. If you do not have a large field in which to practice this task, you can use strategically placed cones in an arena or pasture area. Practice maneuvering around the cones until the horse is light and responsive to your requests.

Winning advantages with your horse in a fair manner does a lot for your relationship with him. He will begin to perceive you as the alpha in the relationship, his attitude will get better, his expression will change, he will become more sensitive to your requests, and often, he will feel a sense of relief. This is because it is a lot less work and worry for the horse when he does not have to play the alpha horse role. Instead, the horse will look to you for leadership and safety.

Your horse's expressions will indicate your success in playing these games. His expressions are communication techniques that give you access to his state of mind. Be aware of these expressions because they will help you succeed.

Expressions from the horse that you might see when you are winning the advantages in a fair manner include the horse

- Having his ears focused on you or softly relaxed
- Blinking
- Softly sighing or sneezing
- Not wrinkling his nostrils
- Licking his lips
- Lowering his head

These positive signs let you know that you were firm but fair, that you were clear in your communication, and that you added appropriate pressure when needed and took the pressure away when you got a good response.

However, just as there are positive signs, you may also see negative signs that show you that you were too firm or unfair in some way. These include the horse

- Pinning his ears back
- Becoming starry-eyed and unblinking
- Wrinkling his nostrils
- Raising his head
- Kicking
- Bolting
- Rearing
- Showing tension in his muscles or movement
- Lacking rhythm in his gait

If you receive negative signs from the horse, it could mean that he did not understand you or that you were unfair, were too firm, or did not release the pressure when the horse responded correctly. This feedback lets you know that you need to make an adjustment in your approach.

CHAPTER 11
Using Phases of Pressure to Accomplish a Task

W̲e want our horses to be responsive to the lightest phases of pressure or the slightest cues possible. To achieve this, we have to become consistent at using a series of cues or phases of pressure in a sequential manner. If we don't learn to start light and only gradually increase phases of pressure or add cues when the horse is not responding, the horse will never learn to be light and responsive.

The horse is very sensitive by nature and can feel the slightest touch on his hair. He may choose to be nonresponsive, but he does feel it. He could also be nonresponsive because he is unsure of the request, is dull from too much stimulus or pressure, believes he is more dominant, or is fearful and not able to think his way to the solution. Usually, the horse shows fear only if we have been too firm, we have moved too fast through a series of cues, our phases of pressure have been too intense or too fast, or we have been unfair. In all these cases, it is up to us to be clear about our requests and add additional cues or pressure only when the request is not met.

A cue is a signal that you give to your horse that encourages him to respond to your request. A cue can come in many forms:

- Taking in a deep breath and bringing up energy in your body to request a certain movement from the horse
- Changing the position of your body to inform the horse to go, stop, or turn

- Providing light leg pressure or a light movement on the rein or reins
- Making a verbal smooch or cluck

You may use a single cue or a sequence of cues to work on getting a particular response from a horse. A phase of pressure is the use of a single cue with a light amount of pressure and additional pressure if the horse is not responding to your request.

When you cue your horse, start out with the least amount of pressure possible. It does not matter what the task is because this works for every task whether you are riding or working on the ground. Begin by adding a light amount of pressure to your cue. If the horse is responsive, take the pressure off immediately, and smile. You can also say, "Good boy" or "Good girl." The horse can feel the emotion that comes with your words. This lets him know you are pleased. However, if the horse does not respond after a couple of seconds, add an additional cue or additional pressure from the same cue to encourage a response. If the horse still does not respond after a couple of seconds, add another cue or more pressure from the same cue again. Pretty soon, the horse will start to realize that if he does not respond, the pressure will intensify, and he will be very uncomfortable.

Horses understand patterns, and after you have done this a few times with consistency, the horse will begin to see and understand the pattern. Your horse will work toward finding a solution to get away from the pressure so he can feel more comfortable. Remember that while you are working on getting a response from your horse, you need to do it without being mean or getting mad at him. You are the teacher, and your horse is the student. He can't learn if the environment is hostile. If you are mean or angry, your horse may end up responding, but he will be reacting out of fear instead of respect. There is a huge difference.

It is important to be able to recognize when the horse is not responding because he is unsure of the proper response or is trying to find the solution. If the horse is trying to figure out what the proper response is supposed to be, he may have an ear and an eye focused on the cue or the pressure that you are offering. He may also raise his head slightly and have a somewhat puzzled look on his face. At this moment, it is important to not add additional phases of pressure but instead to give the horse extra time to figure out exactly what it is that you are asking for. The horse may offer several responses before he finds the right answer. At this moment, just stick with the soft cue phase of pressure and hold it until the horse finds the right answer. When he does, immediately release the pressure, and reward the horse for finding the correct answer.

After the horse has found the right answer, it is important to give him the critical time he needs to stop and reflect on what has just transpired. Let him have time to lower his head and look sleepy, and wait for the blinking and licking of the lips. If you give the horse this time, there will be a better chance that he will respond appropriately the next time you ask for the same thing. Just make sure that you ask with the same cue or phase of pressure.

Lead horses in the wild or in herd situations always use cues or phases of pressure to get the herd to complete a request. When an alpha horse wants to be first to the food, she will let the others know that they have to wait their turn.

The alpha horse may use a series of cues or phases of pressure such as

- Turning her head toward the other horses and pinning her ears back
- Wrinkling her nose
- Pushing with her shoulder
- Swinging her head around
- Turning her hind end toward the others and maybe backing up toward them to push them away
- Nipping
- Kicking
- Rearing

The moment that the alpha horse is effective, she will stop all her cues and go about eating. It is nothing personal. The alpha horse is not mad or upset. She is just communicating. A horseperson must use cues and phases of pressure similar to those of the alpha horse. Next, I list a few examples of cues and phases of pressure that you can use.

Asking for a Walk from a Horse under Saddle with a Sequence of Cues

To go from a halt to a walk under saddle, start with loose reins, and gently lift the reins just a little bit to get your horse's attention. At this point, depending on your comfort level, you can either make light contact with the horse with the reins or keep the reins loose. Now bring up some energy in your body by breathing in and smiling. Using your energy should always be your first phase of pressure because this is the first phase that horses use with one another. If your horse does not start walking after a second or two, lightly squeeze him with your legs, but don't kick. If the horse has not begun to walk forward, add a smooching or kissing noise. If, after another couple of seconds, the horse has not started walking, use a riding crop to make light, rhythmic taps on his shoulder or behind your leg on the back side of the horse's rib cage to encourage him to move forward. The moment your horse begins to walk, take all pressure off, and smile. It is very helpful if you make a walking motion with your own body so that you are moving forward along with the horse. If your horse stops, just ask again in the same manner. Bring up your energy, squeeze with your legs, make a smooching or kissing noise, and then tap with the riding crop. Wait a couple of seconds between each phase to give the horse time to think. Be consistent, and your horse will begin to understand the sequence of phases. Eventually, he will begin to respond to just the energy in your body because he will realize that there are more phases to come if he does not respond. When your horse begins to improve and respond with fewer phases, reward his effort.

Troubleshooting

- If your horse does not respond when you add the tap–tap with the riding crop, you can add a little more pressure to the tap–tap motion. Every couple of seconds, increase the amount of pressure until the horse responds.

- If your horse raises his head and starts moving backward or sideways, just keep lightly tapping until he moves a step forward and then immediately release all pressure. Those wrong movements from the horse are just signs of worry or confusion. The horse may be trying to figure out what it is that you are asking for. If the horse is moving in the wrong direction, just keep asking with a calm and confident attitude until he finds the right answer, and then reward him.

- If your horse takes off too quickly, it just means that you added too much pressure. Calm the horse down by bending him to a stop or doing small circles until he decides to stop. Pet the horse; look for the horse's head to lower, his breathing to relax, and his eyes to blink; and then try again with less pressure.

Phases of Pressure to Lead Your Horse by Your Side on a Lead Line

You can use phases of pressure to lead your horse forward on a lead line with him at your side, shoulder to shoulder. As you walk forward, it will be your horse's job to stay next to your side at all gaits. Begin at a halt with the lead line in the hand that is closest to the horse and a stick and string or lunge whip in your other hand. Keep the lead line slack so the horse does not run into pressure from it right away. You want him to learn to follow you, step by step, without being pulled. First, begin to bring up some energy in your body by taking in a good breath. Then, start to walk, and if your horse does not immediately begin to walk with you, use your lunge whip or stick and string to tap the ground lightly behind the horse. Stay facing and looking forward and keep walking. If he does not respond, tap the ground lightly behind you and the horse several times with some rhythm. Keep tapping the ground with rhythm until the horse begins to walk forward, and then stop the tapping, smile, and walk with the horse. This same thing can also be accomplished by gently touching his hind end with the stick or lunge whip but only if you have a horse that is not very fearful or reactive. You don't want to scare him or get hurt by having him run into you. So, be sure to start with a very light tap on the hind end. The moment he responds, relax the stick or whip in your hand by letting the tail end of the stick or whip drag on the ground next to your side, and smile. Your horse's job is to maintain the walk by your side and keep slack in the lead line until further notice. If you want him to start trotting, take a good breath again, and start trotting with your legs first. Then, use your phases of pressure in the same manner if he does not begin to trot. If you want to go back to a walk, you need to slow the energy down in your body and start walking first; then your horse should begin walking too.

Troubleshooting

- If you are walking forward and your horse does not follow you even after you add pressure with the stick and string or lunge whip, keep walking but turn slightly to the left or right so that you are at either a ten-o'clock or two-o'clock position. The direction change will put the horse slightly off balance, and this will make it harder for him to stand still. Choose the direction that is turning away from the horse. If the horse is on your left side, walk to the right. This should cause the horse to start walking when he feels the lead line pull him off balance. Now smile and walk off together.
- If the horse does not slow down to a lower gait when you request it, put your stick out in front of you, gently wiggle it up and down in front of his nose until he begins to walk, and then take the stick away from the horse, smile, and walk with the horse.
- If, for any reason, the horse breaks gait to a lower gait without you asking for him to do so, just use your phases of pressure again until he responds appropriately.

If you are consistent, you will find that your horse will get into a rhythm with you and stay at the speed and gait that you have chosen. Horses like to be in rhythm and harmony. Once he understands the pattern, your horse will put effort into being in rhythm with you. It will also help if you keep your two feet walking in rhythm with the horse's two front feet. Remember that there is a learning curve here for both of you. So, be patient and persistent in your phases of pressure, and you will begin to see amazing results.

Disengaging the Horse's Hind End while He Is under Saddle with a Sequence of Cues

This example describes moving the horse's hind end while you are in the saddle. Let's start with moving his hind end to the right. Slowly gather up your reins so you have light contact with the horse's mouth, and have a riding crop in your left hand. Slide your left leg back, and gently touch his ribcage with your left calf muscle. Point your toe out, hold your calf muscle steady on his ribcage, and wait for your horse to move his hind legs away from your leg. If he does not respond after a few seconds, lightly tap–tap with a riding crop just behind your left leg. Try not to pull on the reins at the same time. If the horse tries to go forward, just gently stop the forward motion with the reins. If the horse still has not moved the hind legs away after a couple of seconds, pick up the rhythm of the tap–tap motion of the stick. The moment the horse responds, take all pressure off, and reward him with a soft pet and a "good boy" or "good girl." As the horse begins to understand what you want, it should take fewer phases of pressure and less time. If you feel that the horse is trying to figure out what the right response is, don't add additional pressure. Give him a few moments to find the right answer. Once he finds the correct answer, give him a moment to reflect before you ask again. When you begin to ask for more steps, just slightly release your calf muscle momentarily as you get a step, and gently put the calf muscle back on again for another step. Use the stick only when it is needed. Remember that the lighter you can start with your phases, the lighter your horse will be as you advance.

Troubleshooting

- If the horse does not understand your request and starts moving forward or backward, just maintain your position and aids until he gives the proper response, and then reward him.
- If your horse kicks out, it probably means you added too much pressure with the riding crop or your leg.
- If your horse is moving his hind end to the right but the front legs keep moving as well, you might want to use the reins to impede the forward movement.

Be consistent with your cues and phases of pressure, and remember to always start with light pressure and add additional pressure only if it is needed. The quicker you can release pressure when the horse responds appropriately, the quicker the horse will understand the request. Reward the horse for his efforts as much as possible, and help him to feel like a winner. The more often that a horse feels rewarded for his efforts, the more the horse will begin to offer you. I always look for moments to reward horses. It puts the relationship in a positive and progressive state of being.

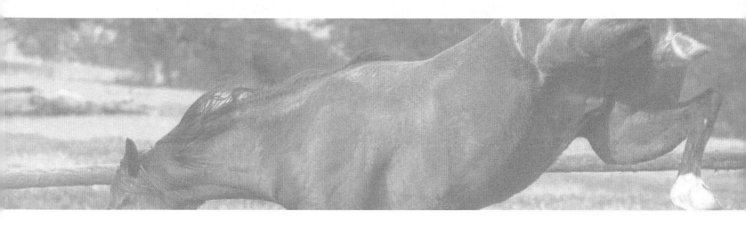

CHAPTER 12
Training Techniques for
Confident and Unconfident Horses

B ecause every horse has his own individual personality, it is important to customize warm-up and training sessions in a way that is appropriate for each horse. Some horses desire more repetition in warm-up and training sessions, and other horses desire more variety. In this chapter, I discuss techniques to customize your sessions to the personality of your horse in order to have more success.

Consistency with the Unconfident Horse

A horse that is more unconfident by nature or a horse that becomes unconfident during a session will most likely need more repetition. It is a good idea to have a warm-up session on a line with this horse before you ride or engage him in the teaching part of your time together. Spend some time with him on a line to see if he is emotionally calm and to determine what you need to do to get him focused on you. It is just as important to get his muscles physically warmed up and ready to engage in more physical activities. He may also have a lot of pent-up energy that he needs to expend before he is ready to act like a partner. Sometimes, these horses like to kick up their heels, run, and buck. I personally would rather this happen on a line than when I am on his back. I will not ride a horse until I know he is mentally connected to me and acting like a partner. If you halter your horse and find that he is quickly responsive and connected to you, a warm-up session while you are riding is fine.

Some of the questions I ask myself during a warm-up to determine whether a horse is mentally connected to me are as follows:

- Does the horse go forward and stop when I ask without getting emotionally worked up?
- Is the horse responsive when I ask him to move his front or hind end around?
- Is the horse's attention on me, or is it elsewhere?
- Is the horse worried, or is he calm and attentive?

You can assess his mental state in the first few minutes that you are with the horse. Feel for where his energy level is and how responsive or unresponsive he is to your requests. If you are in doubt, warm up the horse on a line, and stay safe.

A warm-up session with an unconfident horse while he is on a line or you are riding can be done with patterns such as circles, changes of gait, changes of direction, sideways maneuvers, figure eights, and obstacles. These patterns are a good way to help the horse relax and get in a good learning frame of mind. The more worried and unconfident the horse is, the smaller you should make the circles or figure eights. Circles offer consistency, and the horse can relax better because he realizes that he is not going anywhere and understands the pattern.

If the horse is an unconfident, high-energy horse, he will probably need to do a pattern at a trot or canter and for a longer period of time than a horse with less energy. You may even add some poles, logs, or small jumps to engage his mind and use up his excess energy. A good way to test whether your horse is feeling the need to buck is to send him over a jump. A jump can encourage a horse to buck if he has pent-up energy. I would rather a horse get his bucks out of the way before I ride.

Be careful not to add too many transitions between the walk, trot, and canter with an unconfident horse. You are looking for relaxation in your horse during the warm-up so that he can be calm and in a learning frame of mind. If you find that your horse is becoming bored and unmotivated, add some more changes of gait or change the speed within a gait. Alternatively, if your horse becomes more worried, ask for fewer transitions.

Being observant of your horse's mental and emotional states and adjusting your session to fit his needs are keys to success. You can tell that your horse is relaxed and in a learning frame of mind when you see the following cues:

- The horse's head is relatively low.
- His attention is on you (if he has an ear and eye on you).
- He stays at the speed, direction, and gait you have established.

- He has rhythm in his gait.
- He is responsive to your requests.

Once you see these signs, give the horse a short break as a reward for his efforts. Let him stop, relax, lower his head, and feel good about his efforts. Give him a few moments to reflect and then lick his lips. This will help him remember that being in a good frame of mind is a good thing.

When he starts looking more alert, it is a good time to work on a teaching session if you want to. You can work on new skills, improve a skill that the horse already knows, or play a specific sport. This would also be a good time to go on a trail ride. The key is to have your horse mentally connected to you so that he is a good partner no matter what you decide to do.

If you choose to go on a trail ride, it is important to ask him to stay mentally connected to you. You can accomplish this by doing some transitions, making lateral movements and turns on the forehand and haunches, backing over small obstacles, and so on. If you just mindlessly go on a trail ride, your horse may mentally disconnect from you, and because there is no leadership, he may become more worried or feel that he has to be on guard for potential danger.

When the horse is warmed up and a teaching session begins, present the information slowly enough for him to learn it without feeling too pressured. Keep the session short when the horse is learning something new. Break the task down into small pieces, and teach him one piece at a time. Give him time to fully understand it. Then, you can slowly add more pieces to the task, such as more speed, distance, responsiveness, or precision, or slowly increase its degree of difficulty. If the horse becomes worried or starts bracing his mind and body, this may be an indicator that you are going too fast or putting too much pressure on him. Slow down, and keep your emotions positive so that the horse can learn and think his way through the exercise. Give him time to truly learn what you are trying to teach him at a speed that is appropriate for him. This will give him the confidence to become a super learner and a super partner.

If your horse is learning something new, it is a good idea to repeat the lesson for several sessions. It is hard to say exactly how many because it depends on the degree of difficulty, the horse's confidence and understanding of the task, and your degree of knowledge and teaching ability. The horse will let you know if it is too much, too fast by becoming tense or worried. He will also let you know if he is comfortable with it. Just pay attention to him. He is always trying to give feedback. Be fair, be clear about your goals, and reward every effort.

Troubleshooting

During a session, if your horse begins to worry and his emotions start getting worse, he is probably feeling too much pressure or too much confusion. If he is tense and running around, slow way down, go back to doing something that he knows well, or add some small circles until he can start to relax and come off his adrenaline. Maybe have a small jump or log that the horse can go over while he is doing small circles. When there is an obstacle that the horse has to think about, it often helps him get his brain working again because it causes him to think about where he is placing his feet and doesn't allow him to just run around mindlessly. Make sure that you stay calm and are not amped up along with him. The horse needs you to be calm and focused; he needs your leadership. Once he calms down, just take time to assess and figure out what may have caused his emotional reaction. He may need the information broken down into smaller pieces and probably needs more time to think his way to the right response. Figure out how you can present information to this horse in manageable smaller steps. If the horse is responsive to your request, it is important to take the pressure off and relax the energy in your body. This gives the horse feedback that lets him know you are pleased. There is not one answer to every problem. Every horse is different. Seek help if you need more strategies.

Variety with a Confident Horse

A warm-up session for a confident horse may look a little different than one for an unconfident horse. With a confident horse, you are less likely to be trying to get his emotions to calm down. A confident horse often needs incentives, stimulation, variety, and fun. If he becomes mentally engaged in the warm-up, the rest of the session will go more smoothly.

If he is on a line, have him do transitions between gaits or within a gait, change the size of the circles from large to small and back, add some side passing, change direction, go over poles, do some jumps, and circle him on uneven ground if you can. Be creative. You can do the same thing while you are riding, and you can add some straight lines and use fewer circles.

Oftentimes, circles are too repetitive and bore the confident horse. The horse can lose motivation and get crabby if he has to do too many. Straight lines help confident horses feel as if they are going somewhere.

If you need to motivate a confident horse a little more, add several stopping points to your straight lines. Go straight from one end of the arena to the other, and stop for a couple of seconds; then repeat, and head to another end or corner of the arena before stopping again for a couple more seconds. If you are in an open field or large area with trees and bushes, you can go from one tree, bush, cone, or log to another, stop for a couple of seconds, and then head to a different obstacle and stop. Spend some time stopping at different locations for a few seconds. Treat it as a fun game, and see whether the horse's impulsion comes up and his energy improves.

Frequent transitions between gaits are another great motivator for a confident horse. You can work on transitioning back and forth from a walk to a trot, from a walk to a canter, from a trot to a canter, from a canter to a backup, or from a halt to a canter. Changing the speed within a gait also helps to motivate this horse. Pick a gait such as a trot. Ask the horse for a fast trot for a designated number of steps and then a slow trot for the same number of steps, and just rotate back and forth. You will be surprised to see just how fast your horse picks up on the pattern, and you will also notice that he will start to recognize how many steps he needs to do at each speed. Make it fun, and the horse will have fun. If the horse starts to anticipate the number of steps or where you are going to stop, it is time to mix it up a little so that he does not take over and try to call the shots. Keep enough consistency that the horse understands the pattern, but have enough variety that you keep him looking to you for the answer. It is a balancing act. Have fun with it.

Once you have the horse's motivation up and he is responsive, you can work on a training session, work on a specific sport, or go on a trail ride if you desire. The confident horse can learn faster when the information is presented in a way that he can understand. It is a good idea to repeat the lesson for several days before you add a higher degree of difficulty or other maneuvers if you are teaching something new. The amount of time and the number of days will depend on the degree of difficulty of the task and your degree of knowledge and teaching ability. Listen to your horse, and let him be in charge of how much time he needs. Be fair, be clear about your goals, and reward his efforts.

Troubleshooting

Many confident horses will not put in effort if they do not see the purpose of your session. This type of horse can become resistant, and he may challenge your authority, get bored easily, and wonder why he should do what you are asking. Too much repetition in your session can cause this horse to become bored and unmotivated. He needs you to put more variety in the session. Keep it interesting and fun. Changes in the environment, patterns, or routines help to keep confident horses more engaged in activities. Keep advancing your skills and teaching new things. Make sure that whatever you are working on makes sense to the horse and that there are clear patterns. Horses like to understand what they are doing, so try not to haphazardly go about your time together. Seek help from a reputable natural horseperson if needed.

General Training Tips for All Horses

For all types of horses, if you are trying to teach them something new, break it down into small, learnable pieces, and always let them know when they have done something right. You accomplish this by taking the pressure off when your horse gets the right answer. It does not matter what the task is: moving a body part in a certain direction, going faster or slower, stopping, turning, spinning, or jumping. The moment you get the response you are looking for, just release the pressure momentarily. You can do this by releasing the pressure on a rein or reins, leg, lunge whip, or riding crop. Whatever you use to reinforce your request needs to be released so that he knows he has done the right thing. Many quick, temporary releases are needed when you are teaching any lesson. At the end of a task or lesson, remember to quit when he has done something positive or at least improved a little on the task. Take all pressure off, and give him some time to mentally process the lesson. Part of taking the pressure off the horse includes relaxing your body and your breathing.

Always look for a way to reward a horse instead of punishing him. If your focus is on the positive, it will help increase his motivation and impulsion. Be sure to always add a lot of praise in the form of a "good boy" or "good girl" when the horse is trying. You will be amazed at how much harder the horse will try when he knows that you are pleased.

If a mistake is made by the horse, just keep politely asking until you get the right answer, or hold the pressure until he finds it. Chances are the horse did not understand or was confused in some way. The horse is looking to see how he can find a release of pressure. This is how he knows he has done the right thing. If you happen to miss this important step, your horse will never know when he is right. This is when horses give up, get frustrated, or mentally shut down because they never get to know when they are right. This is the secret to how they learn. It is all about the release of pressure.

If the horse makes a mistake and the pressure is taken off him for any reason, he will not know that it was a mistake. The pressure may have been inadvertently taken off for many different reasons, such as the horseperson trying to correct him by changing something and temporarily releasing the pressure. This is confusing to the horse. He gets a temporary release of pressure followed by more pressure, and this is often followed by negative emotion from the person, so now he is really confused. If this happens to you, don't be too hard on yourself because we all make mistakes. It is a mistake only if you don't learn from it. Just shake it off, pet your horse, and do better next time. Horsemanship is a challenging journey, and you need to be gentle with yourself as you learn. Frustration comes when there are more questions than there are answers. If you keep asking questions and keep learning, eventually it will turn around.

Giving a horse time to stand still and think after a lesson and between tasks is very beneficial for him. Sitting still on his back or standing still next to your horse in a relaxed state of mind and body for a few minutes will give him time to process the task or lesson. This pause gives both of you undemanding time together. So, don't just put your horse away the moment you are done. Spend several minutes just being still and letting him absorb the lesson. During these few minutes of undemanding dwelling time, you may notice your horse lower his head and either partially close his eyes or completely close his eyes and begin to look sleepy. This is how a horse begins to process his lesson. The intensity of the lesson and the individual personality of the horse will determine how long he remains looking sleepy. It may be only a minute or two, or it may be ten minutes, thirty minutes, or longer. The more intense the session was for the horse, the longer the dwelling time could be.

If the horse is having trouble relaxing or does not start looking sleepy at this point, assess the situation. There may be many different reasons that your horse is not relaxing and thinking. There may have been too much pressure put on him and his brain is locked up, he may not have gotten the meaning of the session, or he may not have learned anything new in the time you spent together. Sometimes, the energy in your body may still be up, or you're still holding a little tension. If this happens, try relaxing your muscles, loosening your shoulders, turning the front of your body away from your horse, slowing your breathing down, and taking your eyes off him. These are all ways to take pressure off your horse. It is also a good idea not to pet your horse during his dwelling time; it just distracts him and may even annoy him. Just be there with him. Then your horse can feel as if the pressure is off, and he can relax and dwell. When your horse is in the process of reviewing the lesson he just had, you will probably see some of the following signs from him:

- The horse lowers his head.
- He blinks, rolls his eyes, and looks sleepy.
- He sneezes and rubs his nose on a front leg.
- He yawns and licks his lips.
- He shakes his neck or whole body as he would after a good roll.
- He may even want to roll on the ground.

If the lip licking is fast or if your horse is sneezing fast and tight, there is still tension in him. If your horse is licking his lips slowly or he is softly sneezing, he is thinking and processing information. In this case, be mindful, and give him time to process the session. It will do wonders for your relationship.

These are all signs that you can find with any type of horse. It may take longer for an unconfident horse to express these signs because his emotions have to come down first, and he has to feel comfortable in your presence. Once your horse displays these signs and starts looking more alert, it is a good time to pet him and tell him how wonderful he is. Begin with love, add love in the session, and end with love.

CHAPTER 13
How to Help Your Horse
Become More Confident

Some horses are born more curious by nature than others. If you have a herd of horses that is introduced to something new, you will see that some will naturally want to get closer and find out what it is. There are others that will want nothing to do with it and will have no interest at all, and others that will be terrified. Our job is to help our horses gain confidence and become more curious. Curiosity builds confidence.

As people, we are responsible for many unnatural obstacles that can bother a horse, including plastic bags, bicycles, motorcycles, guns, balloons, sirens, umbrellas, and horse trailers. We need to get into the habit of looking at each obstacle that we encounter with our horse as a stepping-stone for building his confidence instead of a problem that needs to be solved. Once we get into that habit, these encounters become learning experiences filled with patience and understanding. If we just get mad at the horse because he is worried, unconfident, or fearful, he will never learn how to be a confident partner for us. The horse will never learn how to trust us and how to overcome his fears. If we learn how to help the horse to overcome his fears and teach him that he can trust us to help him, he can be the partner we have always dreamed of.

We are the teachers, and the horses need to learn to trust us. They can't do that if we get frustrated or mad at them. It is important that we as teachers develop a set of ideas, concepts, and actions to help promote the positive outcome we are looking for in our horses. If we have a plan and know what to do when our horses are afraid or unconfident, we can avoid getting angry and frustrated.

When you do lose your patience, it is best to take a break with your horse and calm down. This break can preserve your relationship.

While you are taking a break, you can seek out different solutions. Maybe you have a natural horsemanship trainer you can turn to, a video you can watch, articles you can read, or a friend who may have positive suggestions. Maybe there are some answers in this book. Just don't give up. The more knowledge you gain and the more obstacles you overcome, the better teacher and leader you will be for your horse. Be patient with yourself. Learning good horsemanship takes time. Every good horseperson out there has been through this.

Make sure that whatever advice you take feels good in your heart. Don't compromise your relationship with your horse just to get something done. It will not feel good to you, and it will not feel good to your horse.

Introducing Your Horse to a Scary Object

Horses typically become nervous when they see something that is unfamiliar to them. As prey animals, they have instincts telling them to be on alert and to be fearful of any changes in the environment, such as things that pop out of the bushes or show up around corners, and pretty much anything unknown. So, it is our duty to help them overcome their fears so they can become braver and fit into our world. Often, we will wonder why something as simple as a plastic bag can make a horse panic. We know that the plastic bag is harmless, but the horse does not.

It can be a pretty simple task to introduce a new object to a horse when this is done correctly. Let's start with the plastic bag. Here are a few ways to build your horse's confidence. Start by retreating away from your horse with the plastic bag. You can do this by facing the horse and walking backward. Have him on a long lead line, and let him follow you and the bag as you move away from him. If he does not want to follow, maybe the bag is still too close to him, is making too much noise, or is too big. Help your horse by starting with the plastic bag bundled up into a smaller size or by making sure that the bag makes less noise. Just start with less intensity, and build his confidence one step at a time.

As your horse gets more confident, you can slowly add more intensity. It is a good idea to have some slack in the long lead line and find the distance that is comfortable for your horse so that he becomes curious and wants to follow. This may be five feet, or it may be twenty feet or more. You let your horse decide how much space he needs between the plastic bag and himself. Make sure the lead line is long enough to allow the horse to find his comfort level. You can use a lunge line that is twenty feet long or longer to set this task up for success. Begin by walking away from the horse and allowing more slack in the lead rope or lung line. This will start to pique some of the horse's curiosity, and he will begin to want to follow the plastic bag. You may want to walk a little to the left or right of the horse. This might help him begin to move his feet. If an object is going away from a horse, it is not seen as a big threat.

Another option is to get help from a friend. Having help sometimes allows the task to become a little easier. You hold the lead rope, and have your friend walk ahead of you backward and away from both of you with the plastic bag in hand. The bag can be in your friend's hand or tied to the end of a stick. Start with the bag bundled up small but big enough for the horse to see. Have your friend walk away from him until the horse starts becoming curious. If he wants to come up and smell it, that is great, but don't let him bite the bag. If the horse starts to get worried, just use a smaller bag, and have your friend make less noise with it. You can also slow down or put more distance between the horse and the bag. Stay calm, and support the horse's efforts. Once he is OK with the balled up plastic bag, you can gradually make the bag bigger. Just remember, every time you change the size of the bag or begin to let it make more noise, you need to start the process all over again by having your friend retreat away from the horse and having the horse walk toward them. Keep this up until your horse is not worried any longer.

You can revisit this task the next day to determine whether your horse has any remaining concern. This often takes several sessions. If you still see signs of fear, just repeat the task again until he is no longer worried. If you were successful the day before, on the second day, it should take only a fraction of the time to get the horse confident again. Continue this process for several days or weeks just to make sure there is no worry left.

Some Signs That Your Horse Is Scared of the Plastic Bag or Object of Choice

Facial Expressions

- The horse's head is high and may bob up and down.
- His ears are flickering around a lot or are locked on the scary object.
- His eyes are wide and unblinking.
- His nostrils are flared, or he is snorting loudly.

Body Expressions

- The horse can't stand still, bolts, or runs off.
- He has an irregular gait or movement.

- His muscles are tight.
- He rears up, bucks, kicks, or spooks.
- His tail is high.
- He paws at the ground (this can show confusion or frustration).
- He jumps in place and then freezes.
- He freezes in place, gets introverted, and seems not to be able to think.

Some Signs That Your Horse Is Becoming Curious about the Plastic Bag

Facial Expressions

- The horse's head is low.
- His ears are focused on the object. If the ears are not on the object any longer, he has lost interest in the object or has found something else more interesting at the moment.
- His eyes are blinking and soft.
- He has relaxed breathing, is smelling the object, is sneezing softly, or is rubbing his nose on his front leg.
- He is licking his lips.

Body Expressions

- The horse is shaking his neck or whole body to release tension.
- He is walking toward the object.
- He is pawing at the object if it is on the ground.
- He is notably relaxed with a lack of tension.

Anytime you see signs that the horse is becoming curious or less worried, reward the horse by stopping the bag's movement and noise momentarily. This will help teach the horse that if he relaxes a little bit, the plastic bag will become quiet. Rewarding him in this way is another way to release pressure on the horse. The braver the horse becomes, the less threatening the bag will be. After a few moments, you can put the plastic bag back in motion. Then, stop it again when the horse shows another positive sign of relaxation or curiosity. Once the horse is OK with the size of the plastic bag and the noise you are making, you can increase the intensity a little bit. Then just repeat the same steps until there are signs of relaxation again.

This method of allowing a horse to follow a perceived threat from a distance can be done with any object that you want to introduce him to. Start with a comfortable distance that the horse feels is manageable with low-intensity movement and noise, and slowly build up the intensity as your horse gains confidence. Take as long as the horse needs to be OK with it. Try not to put a timeline on how long it should take; let the horse tell you when he is accepting and ready to move forward. The more you watch for the signs listed previously and the more you respond appropriately, the faster your horse will gain confidence in the object and in your leadership.

Another fun obstacle to introduce to a horse is an umbrella. Start with the umbrella closed, and use the same process. Give him a moment to walk toward it and smell it if he wants to. Then slowly start walking away from the horse and add a little twirling motion to the umbrella, or begin opening it just a little bit at a time as you are walking away. Use rhythm, and begin to open it a little, close it, and repeat. If the horse gets too worried, you can slow it down and decrease the intensity. If the horse starts coming toward the umbrella, allow him to approach it again, and stop the umbrella's motion temporarily so he can smell it if he wants to. Then walk away and repeat. Only when the horse is curious should you begin to open the umbrella a little bit more. Remember to increase the intensity of the task only after your horse has accepted the umbrella where you last had it. If you open the umbrella too much and your horse starts to panic, you can always decrease the size, movement, or amount of stimulus to something that is more tolerable. Again, be creative, and look for stimuli around the house or barn for practicing this method with the horse. Both you and the horse will benefit from it.

Introducing a horse to a new object can also be done without a lead line. You can have your horse in an arena or a round pen, and you can start at a distance from the horse that is comfortable for him. Begin walking away from him with the object, and wait for him to begin following you. Start with low-intensity movement and less noise, and make the object smaller if possible. If your horse is worried and does not want to follow you, use even smaller movements and less noise. While you are walking away, it may help if you are facing the horse and walking backward so you can watch for changes in him. This way, you can be quick to reward him or quick to lessen the intensity of the object. It is important to remember that anytime you see signs of curiosity, you should stop all motion from the object for a few moments as a reward for his efforts. Then slowly start walking away with the object, and begin again.

Touching the Horse with Various Objects

If you have an object that you want to be able to touch a horse with or have him wear, you can start with the same process. Retreat with the object in the same way that I described in the last section for the umbrella and the plastic bag. Once your horse is comfortable with the object moving around him and is willing to smell it, you can advance forward, softly rub him with it for a moment or two, take it away for a moment, and then follow the same process again.

Start by touching the horse with the object around the shoulder area first. Rub the shoulder, and if there are signs of relaxation, just take it away for a few moments, and repeat the process. If there is relaxation, you can work your way along his back and rib cage. Save the face for last since it is the most sensitive. Look for signs of relaxation in the horse, and anytime you see him begin to relax, take the object away from him for a few moments as a reward for his efforts. Use rhythm while approaching and retreating with the object over and over until you see some relaxation.

Some Signs of Relaxation to Look For

Facial Expressions

- The horse's head is low.
- His ears are softly focused on the object.
- His eyes are blinking and soft.
- His breathing is relaxed, and he is smelling the object, sneezing softly, and maybe rubbing his nose on his front leg.
- He is licking his lips.

Body Expressions

- The horse's back leg is cocked.
- There is no tension in his body.

These are a few signs of acceptance. At this point, it is good to take the object away from him, and give him a few minutes to process this new information. You will see him lower his head and partially or fully close his eyes. Do nothing except relax and turn your body away from him until he begins to blink, lick his lips, and maybe even yawn. He may sneeze, shake his body as he does after a roll on the ground, and maybe even want to roll on the ground. This is a release of tension. If your horse is unconfident by nature, he may lick his lips without opening his mouth, almost secretly.

Once your horse has finished processing the lesson in his mind, you can advance again, or you can call it a day and give him and yourself a break. If you decide to continue, just continue in the same manner. Don't always expect him to pick up just where you left off. You may have to start with some distance again between the horse and the object and slowly work on advancing closer. Your horse will let you know at what distance he can handle the object. If you have to start again further away, it should take only a fraction of the time to advance to where you had left off before. Take your time again, and slowly get to where he can handle the object touching him.

Troubleshooting

If, at any point during this process, your horse becomes afraid of an object and tries to take off, just do your best to hold onto the rope and minimize the distance he can travel. You may need to put a little more space between him and the object. You may have advanced too quickly. If this is the case, just start again at a distance the horse can handle. You have not failed. This is a learning process for both of you. Be careful not to get rope burn if he is trying to escape. It is better to let go if you can't stop him. Practice in an arena or fenced area so that your horse can't go too far.

If he does get away, drop your object, calmly get your horse, and pet him. You don't want to get mad at the horse; he is doing only what Mother Nature tells him to do. If you get mad, he will lose trust in you and will not want to participate.

Now slowly work on reapproaching the object with a few steps toward the object, a few steps away, and then a few steps forward again until he is back by the object again. If the horse does not want to get too close to the object, just put more slack in the lead line, and start at a distance that the horse can handle. Once you figure out where your horse is in his acceptance of the object and at what distance from the object he needs to be, start the process again by walking away with the object and having the horse start to follow it again. Give the horse as much distance as he needs from the object, and slowly work on improving his confidence in approaching the object again.

Some horses need a lot of time for this process, and others will breeze through it pretty quickly. It may help to zigzag your horse's way back to the object instead of having him move straight toward it. Every horse is different, and we need to treat them as such.

If you begin to get frustrated, find a good moment of success or relaxation to stop, and pick it back up on another day. It is better to take a break and not take it out on your horse. Otherwise, he might take the negative emotion you are feeling and associate it with the object. Just understand that it might take one session, or it might take ten or more. It depends on your horse's ability to confidently work through his fears. It also depends on whether your horse is confident by nature or unconfident. Furthermore, it takes skill from you. If your skill level is low, it will take a lot longer. If your timing of the forward advance to and backward retreat from the object is not timed to the horse's positive or negative responses, it will take longer. There is a learning curve, and you have to be patient with both yourself and your horse.

Crossing a Ditch

Horses have very poor depth perception. You may come across a ditch that is only a few feet wide and a few inches deep, but your horse stops, snorts at it, and refuses to cross it. You may be wondering why he is making such a fuss because it is not that big of a ditch, but he does not know how deep it is. If you remember to look at it from the horse's point of view, you can begin to help him.

Ditch crossing can be accomplished while the horse is on a lead line or while you are riding; this depends on your comfort level and abilities. When your horse reaches the limit on how close he believes he can get to the ditch, you can confidently express to him that he is OK by staying calm and rubbing him on the neck. Next, you can back away from the ditch a little way and watch for the moment when the horse starts to lower his head and relax his breathing. Once he does that, you have permission to reapproach the ditch. Take note of how close he was to the ditch before you retreated. If you can see the hoofprints that he left the first time he approached the ditch, it will be a big help.

As you are reapproaching the ditch, look straight ahead to where you want him to go and not at the ditch. Use some calm, confident energy in your body, and head for the other side of the ditch. If you have a riding crop, lunge whip, or stick and string, you can add a little light, rhythmic tap–tap motion on his shoulder or behind his rib cage to encourage forward motion. Your goal is to get him to go just a little closer than he did the first time. If you need to add some motivating pressure, such as tapping with a riding crop, use your phases of pressure, as discussed in Chapter 11, and once he starts advancing, take the pressure away immediately and allow him to approach. This means taking away leg pressure, stick pressure, rein pressure, and any clucking or kissing noises as well as any negative thoughts. Your horse feels all of it, and he needs the release of all that pressure so that he can think. Once he has advanced a little further than the first time, even if it is just a tiny bit, reward your horse for any and all efforts. If the horse wants to paw at the ground or smell around the ditch, that is OK; just give him enough rein or lead line to explore. Once again, retreat after the horse has advanced toward the ditch. This helps build his confidence. He needs to know that you are not going to push him too far past his comfort zone.

Every time he puts in a little effort, it is good to reward him for his effort with a "good boy" and a pet on the neck. Repeat this as many times as it takes. Don't be in a hurry. You are there to help him gain confidence and learn that he can overcome his fears. If your horse is observing the ditch or pawing at the ground, just relax in your body temporarily. This will give him time to figure it out without any added energy coming from you. Look for moments when you can reward the horse instead of focusing on pushing or punishing him. You still may have to add some pressure to motivate the horse, but your focus should be on the horse's moments of trying. If we allow the horse time to think and try on his own, when the moment comes that he decides to cross the ditch, it will be his decision to do it, and this will be meaningful to him.

If you find you are losing your patience or your horse's fear and adrenaline are coming up, it would benefit both you and your horse if you took a break and tried again later. Just find a positive moment of trying from your horse, and then quit for the day. No good can come from a session full of negative emotions. It will ruin your horse's confidence and your rapport with him, and it will not be better the next day.

If you didn't make it across the ditch on the first day, but you made progress and he got closer, that is OK. It is still progress. Remember that you are both learning and that it may take a little more time. The better your skills get, the faster it will happen in the future. Horsemanship is a journey, and the best horsemen never quit learning and improving. This is not about getting your horse across the ditch at any cost. This is about teaching your horse that he can trust you and that he can overcome his fears with your help and guidance.

CHAPTER 14
How Your Emotions and Body Energy Affect Your Horse

When you are in the presence of a horse, your emotional state is very important. Horses are extremely perceptive to our emotions, and they can tell whether our emotions are positive or negative. The horse may not understand the reasoning behind your emotions, but he knows whether they are good or bad. He is aware of our emotions the moment he sees us. Of course, some horses are more perceptive, and some are more sensitive to a person's emotional state than others. Some horses have been misunderstood for so long that they have learned to ignore or become numb to people's emotions. This can be corrected with knowledge and understanding.

Horses are prey animals and depend on the herd for survival. Their lives might depend on paying attention to the emotions of other horses. The horseperson is part of the herd as well, so your emotions matter. If you are approaching your horse and his head is down and he is grazing or just relaxing, you may think he is not paying attention to you. However, if he has one or both ears pointed toward you, he is already picking up on your emotional state. The horse is watching and observing your body language, tension, emotions, and intentions.

I have witnessed some of my own students looking tense or uptight when they were getting ready for a lesson. For example, a couple of weeks ago, I drove up to a student's ranch, and as I got out of the car, I noticed tension in my student as she was saddling up her horse. Her movements were stiff, she sounded irritable, and she was getting the horse ready quickly without watching for his expressions. I asked her how she was doing, and she explained to me how she had had a challenging morning before she got to the barn and how her horse was not behaving properly. I knew that her horse's behavior was related to her mood, so I had her stop what she was doing so she could take a couple of deep, relaxing breaths. I then asked her to stop and listen to the birds singing in the trees. Next, I had her think of three things she was thankful for. After a few minutes, I saw the tension in her go away, and her horse let out a big sigh. We ended up having a great lesson, which ended with her giggling with lots of joy over her success. Her horse was relaxed and happy right along with her. Our attitude and emotions are so important to our horses.

Intentions also play a big role in being a good leader for your horse. Intention is an act of mental focus to bring a desired response into action in a respectful manner matched with a strong desire to carry it through. Your horse can sense your feelings of intention. When your intention is clear, your horse's response will eventually match your desired intention as long as it is brought about in a respectful manner. When you approach his stall, the horse knows when you have a plan for your time together, and he knows when you don't. Plan ahead of time so you have a purpose for your session together. However, if something goes wrong, such as the horse becoming confused or fearful, it is important to put the plan on hold long enough to help the horse gain clarity or confidence.

Next, I list some of our own expressions and mental states that our horses can pick up on.

Your Negative Body Expressions or Movements

- Staring at your horse
- A tight jaw
- Tension in your body or tight movements in your shoulders, arms, back, hips, and legs
- Acting like a predator by walking straight at your horse

Your Mental States

- Tense thoughts, a bad attitude, anger, frustration, displeasing thoughts, anxiety, or feelings of sadness or fear
- A lack of awareness of your horse's emotional state
- A lack of being fully present in the moment with your attention and thoughts elsewhere
- A lack of a plan for the time you spend with your horse

It does not matter if you are riding a horse, working with a horse on the ground, catching a horse, or just going to visit him. The horse is always observing to see if you or anything in his environment is a threat to him. Negative emotions are seen as a threat, so check your emotional state before you go see your horse and while you are working and playing with him. If you happen to be working with a horse and he is not responding the way you wish and you are becoming angry or frustrated, it will make it very hard for him to concentrate and learn. Chances are that the horse either is trying to do what you have asked or is confused, scared, or unsure about the request.

We have a tendency to think that our horses must understand what we want and that they are just acting badly. This misunderstanding is often what gets the relationship that we have with our horses in so much trouble. We often have a hard time reading and understanding our horses' body language and all their gestures, and they have a hard time understanding what is expected of them and what exactly we are asking of them. They also might not feel as if they are fulfilling our requests because they are not getting the release of pressure when they do the right thing. There is no way for a horse to know that he is doing the right thing if there is no release of pressure. This confusion may lead the horse to quit trying, give up, or just shut down emotionally and physically.

Do You Have True Relaxation in Your Body?

When you are relaxed in your body, it sends a message to the horse that you are not a threat, you are happy to be in the horse's presence, or you are happy with the horse's response to your recent request. The horse is always looking for clues to indicate whether the situation is good or bad. So, being relaxed and feeling pleased is one way to feel successful with your time together. Many times, we think we are relaxed because we are standing still, but if you do a body check on yourself, you may find that there is tension somewhere in your body. You may not be aware of all the ways that there can be tension in your body, but your horse is aware. Remember that your horse is very perceptive. Any signs of tension in your body send a message to your horse that there is some type of threat to worry about.

Ask yourself if you are truly relaxed. Do a body check from top to bottom. Stand up straight, pause for a moment, and then check the following:

- Is your facial expression soft?
- Are your mouth and jaw relaxed?
- Is your breathing relaxed?
- Are your shoulders relaxed and low?
- Are your elbows and hands relaxed?
- Is your spine relaxed? (Bending one knee will help.)

Make it a habit to start from the top of your body, and work your way down to check for signs of tension. If you find tension anywhere in your body, just change it. It is that simple. You can perform the same relaxation exercise while you are in motion. Just check your body parts, and also make sure that there is a soft rhythm in your motion.

Approaching a Horse

As you are walking toward your horse, just as I discussed in the last section, do a quick body check, and make sure you are relaxed in your muscles as well as in your thoughts. Try not to stare at your horse or walk straight up to his head. These are signs of pressure to the horse. Walk confidently and without tension toward the horse's shoulder area instead. Keep your eyes soft, and have a smile on your face. Present your hand to the horse with the palm facing down, and allow him to smell the top side of your hand. If he smells your hand, you have permission to pet him and halter him. If he does not smell your hand or he turns his head away, the horse is not confident, is worried, or may be distrusting. You can read more about this in Chapter 8, "Greeting and Haltering Your Horse."

Horses Pay Attention to Your Current Energy Level and State of Mind

Have you ever gone to ride your horse after a long hard day when you knew you were exhausted but you wanted to ride anyway, and you felt that your horse had the same lack of energy you did? Or maybe you went out for a ride after work and were superexcited to have time to be with your horse and you found that his energy was pretty good that day too?

Well, surprisingly enough, horses pick up on the energy, or the lack of energy, that you are putting out. Similar things may happen during a horse-riding clinic with several horses and riders. You may trailer out to meet a group of riders and find that your normally pretty relaxed horse is now pretty anxious. Then you look around and realize the other horses and riders are having the same problem. What may actually be happening is that your horse is picking up on the anxiety of the other horses and/or people, your anxiety, or a combination of these. That is what horses do in herd situations, in group situations, or with just the two of you.

This is survival to him. He pays attention to the emotions of those around him, and if the emotions are negative, he will be prepared to respond as if there is danger. For this reason, it is very important to have a good handle on your emotions when you're around horses.

If your horse is not used to being out of his normal environment and you take him to new surroundings, he may be genuinely worried. Many horses do feel unconfident outside familiar surroundings. If this is the case, it will be even more important for you to have a handle on your emotions so that the horse can look to you for leadership.

In this type of situation, I will not ride my horse until I know that he is emotionally calm, mentally connected with me, and responsive to my requests. I prefer to use mentally engaging groundwork to get my horse prepared to ride. This can come in the form of circling my horse on a long line over uneven ground or jumps, changing direction, making the circle larger and smaller, or changing the speed within a certain gait. This helps me engage his mind and not just his body. I might also send him backward and sideways and make sure I have control of the forehand and hind end. I want him to be responsive to me and my requests and to be less reactive to his new surroundings. If the horse is an unconfident horse, I will do more small circles and backing and fewer transitions. I will wait until the horse is acting like a partner and is connected to me mentally before I decide that he is OK to ride. You can also build your own self-confidence as a rider in this manner.

Here are some questions to ask yourself to determine whether your horse is calm and mentally engaged with you:

Facial Expressions

- Is the horse's head relatively low?
- Are his ears attentive to you?
- Are his eyes blinking and soft looking with no visible whites?
- Are both of his nostrils the same size, or is he sneezing softly?
- Does he reach his nose out to smell your hand?
- Is he licking his lips or yawning?

Body Expressions

- Is the horse's gait rhythmic and smooth, and does he maintain speed and direction?
- Is he responsive to your requests?
- Is his tail flowing slowly with no tight swishes?
- Is there a lack of tension in the muscles of his body?

If the answers to these questions are yes, you are heading in the right direction. These expressions indicate that your horse is positively engaged with you. Learning to recognize and read these signs can give you the information that you need to know whether your horse is ready to learn, ready to be ridden, or ready for whatever endeavor you choose to work on.

Changing Gaits by Using Your Body Energy while You Are Riding

Horses are also very good at tuning into the energy level in your body during a ride. Let's say that you are riding your horse at a walk, and you would like him to trot. Instead of kicking him to go, try to bring up the same amount of energy in your body that you would use if you were trotting on your own two feet, and take a good deep breath and smile. This may be hard at first, but keep trying, and make sure that the energy that you are bringing up in your body is positive. If your horse does not respond, you can try lightly squeezing with your calf muscles. If that does not work after a couple of seconds, smooch or cluck, and keep the leg pressure on. If he still has not responded after a couple of more seconds, use a riding crop, and gently tap him on the shoulder or tap him behind the ribcage with a consistent, soft tap–tap–tap rhythm while still keeping your energy up and your legs on him. The moment he begins to trot, take off all pressure from your aids, but keep the energy up in your body, and smile. If you repeat this series of steps in the same order every time, your horse will begin to see the pattern and will soon respond to just the energy that you bring up in your body. If he breaks gait, ask again in the same manner. When you first begin this process, it will take some time for your horse to understand exactly what it is that you are asking, especially if the horse is used to being kicked and whacked to go. With consistent repetition, it won't take too long for the horse to understand the new pattern. Once he understands and begins to respond to the energy that you bring up in your body, the resistance that he used to show will change, and he will respond with a much more positive attitude.

Here are the four steps for increasing gait:

1. Bring up energy in your body by breathing in and feeling positive.
2. Gently squeeze the horse with your calf muscles.
3. Make a smooching or clucking noise.
4. Lightly tap the horse with your riding crop on the shoulder or behind the ribcage with a consistent rhythm.

Plan on having about two seconds between each of these four steps so that the horse can understand the pattern. When your horse does trot, you want your lower body from the hips down to move in harmony with his movement. Just follow the movement of your horse or post the trot by only lightly touching the saddle with your seat, and you will feel more harmonious. If you sit too hard in the saddle, it is hard on the horse's back and also hard to stay in rhythm.

If you want your horse to slow down to a walk, bring the energy in your body down slightly to the amount of energy you would have if you were walking on your own two feet, and breathe a little more slowly. If the horse does not slow down, lift up on one rein in a gentle manner, and have your thumb pointed up. The moment the horse walks, release the pressure on the rein so he knows that he has done the right thing. Remember to keep walking energy in your body. If you are riding with two reins, lighten the rein pressure slightly as a reward.

You would do the same thing if you wanted him to stop. First, you take the walking energy out of your body, exhale, and stop riding. Just relax your body and legs, and slow down your breathing. If he does not respond, hold one rein and gently lift it upward until he stops, then release all pressure in the reins, and pet him. Eventually, he will learn to respond to just the energy in your body. Whether you are trying to speed up or slow down, the energy in your body can greatly enhance your riding experience. It can also begin to feel and look like a dance between you and your horse. Your horse will also be much happier when you are part of the dance.

Here are the four steps to slow down the gait:

1. Slow your breathing down.
2. Change your body rhythm to the lower gait or stop riding for a halt.
3. Lift one rein gently upward.
4. Release the rein pressure the moment the horse responds.

Remember to wait about two seconds between each of the first three steps to give the horse time to think and understand your requests.

Visualization of the task you want completed can also play a big role in the amount of success you have with your horse. If you have a mental picture of your task at hand and you can see each step in your mind one by one as you are executing it, it will help you and your horse to be more focused. Riding around aimlessly can make you and your horse feel lost without a purpose. Be clear, use patterns, have a picture in your mind, be focused on the present moment, and your results will improve.

Lunge-Line Challenge Using Your Body Energy and Intention

Here is an exercise to practice with your horse to explore your energy and intent. Let's say that you want your horse to do a twenty-meter circle on a lunge line. When you ask your horse to go, bring up the energy in your body by taking in a deep breath, and stand tall and proud. Then slowly begin to point your finger in the direction in which you want the horse to go. If the horse is already facing in a certain direction, you can set him up for success by asking him to go in that direction. Have a strong focus of intention and a smile. Have a specific gait in mind, such as the trot. If the horse complies with the request, relax your body, breath normally, keep smiling, and stand still. Have in mind how many laps you would like the horse to travel, but don't ask for too many. Maybe two to four at first. Allow him to continue in a circle with you standing still in the center of the circle. Stay still and relaxed in your body and thoughts as long as the horse maintains the gait and direction that you have asked for. If the horse breaks gait or changes direction, just ask again in the same manner. Don't correct the horse or add more pressure if the horse is successfully fulfilling your request. If you maintain pressure or put additional pressure on the horse after he goes into a trot, he has no way of knowing that he is doing what you want. The horse is going to understand that he is doing the right thing only if you take off all pressure, emotional and physical, the moment he responds correctly.

Troubleshooting the Lunge-Line Challenge

If the horse does not go into a trot when you ask, you can add more cues in sequential order. First, bring up your body energy and intention, and softly point your finger in the direction you want him to go. If he does not respond after a couple of seconds, add an additional cue from a lunge whip or a stick and string by tapping the ground behind him three or four times in a row in a rhythmic manner. Remember to tap–tap–tap with light taps and not hard whacks. This light tap–tap–tap with the stick is a consequence with good intentions behind it. Whipping or whacking pressure toward the horse comes with more force and negative emotion, and horses know the difference. Also, there has to be a sequence of cues for the horse to realize that if he does not respond to the lightest cue, there will be additional pressure to come. If you begin this way, you will get a horse that becomes lighter and softer with his responses as time goes on. Always start with the lightest amount of pressure with your cues, and increase it only if the horse is unresponsive.

Sometimes, the horse appears unresponsive, but if you look more closely, you might realize that he is thinking and trying to figure out what you want. If he is confused and trying to understand what you are asking, his head may be slightly raised, he may not blink or may blink slowly, his nostrils may be slightly flared, and there may be a puzzled look on his face. If you believe that your horse is confused, slow down, and don't add any additional pressure from your cue. Give the horse a moment to think as you keep light pressure on him. Usually, within a few moments, the horse will try to move in the direction that you want. If the horse's guess is wrong, just politely keep asking with light pressure until he finds the right answer.

It is important not to take the light pressure off until the horse responds appropriately. Otherwise, he will think that the mistake he made was indeed the right answer. If you find that the horse is getting more worried, you can decrease the amount of pressure a little bit, and find a way to present your request more clearly so that the horse can find the answer. This is actually a learning moment for the horse, and as soon as the horse responds correctly, take all pressure off him. The moment you take the pressure off him is the moment he understands that he has responded correctly.

If you have a sensitive horse, starting with light pressure is very important. You can ask the sensitive horse to go out on a twenty-meter circle in the same manner as the confident horse, but you need to be light and polite. If the horse becomes overreactive, he is probably scared, and you will need to make sure that you are not too tense and decrease the pressure even more. If the horse feels that you were unfair with your phases of pressure, he might even kick out at you, pin his ears, bolt, or rear up. This is feedback from the horse to let you know that you may need to slow down or be less firm.

If your horse is nonresponsive or sluggish, you may need to do some troubleshooting. You may need to figure out whether he is bored from too much repetition, there is a lack of leadership or respect, or he is perhaps in pain. There can be many reasons. Sometimes, getting help from a knowledgeable natural horseperson can do a world of good. There is no one answer for every problem. Every situation is unique, and understanding horses from their point of view is key to having a good partnership.

It is important to make circling your horse on a long line intriguing for him. Have him circle on uneven ground or transition between gaits or speeds within a gait, or include poles or jumps to make it more fun. Also, don't do so many circles that you drive your horse crazy. If the horse is light and responsive or shows some improvement, stop, and reward the horse. This will help him feel like a winner. If you do the task too long, he'll lose enthusiasm and become dull. When he completes a task with improvement and feels rewarded, he will be happy and more willing to try again next time. Ask for little bits of improvement daily. A small amount of improvement a day adds up to a lot of improvement over time. Then, you can move on and do something different and fun with your horse.

CHAPTER 15
Balancing Leadership Skills,
Love for Your Horse, and Communication

A true partnership with your horse requires balancing the love you have for your horse, good leadership skills, and clear communication that the horse can understand. This means that if any of these partnership attributes are out of balance, the relationship is out of balance.

Love

Love is doing what is right for the horse. It includes building the horse's confidence, building rapport between the two of you, being a good leader, and always acting in a way that builds trust and confidence in you and your horse. Love also comes in the form of softly petting your horse, taking pressure off the horse at appropriate times, gently grooming your horse, exhibiting positive body language and energy, having a soft heart, greeting your horse by letting him smell your hand with the palm down (the horseman's handshake), and performing any genuine act of kindness.

Sometimes, love just comes in the form of spending undemanding time together. You can spend time with your horse by doing simple things such as sitting in a chair by him and maybe reading a book or listening to music. You can give your horse a massage and maybe some extra treats just for fun.

The horse knows whether he is genuinely loved or is just an object a person uses to reach their personal goals. If ego is more important to someone than doing right by the horse, he will know it, feel it, and hold the person accountable.

Leadership

Leadership can come in the form of having a clear focus and a plan. Focus includes looking where you are going, being observant, and being able to be completely present in every moment with your horse. Horses live in the moment, but you cannot expect them to be any more focused in the present moment than you are. Have a plan for the session, but be willing to change the plan if the horse is having trouble in any area. Good leadership also includes mutual respect (which has to be earned), control of your energy and emotions, appropriate pressure at the appropriate time, and correct timing of the release of pressure, among other things.

Furthermore, leadership involves understanding how to build a horse's confidence and how to help your horse through worry and fear. The horse needs to be able to trust you and your judgment. He needs to know that you will not put him in harm's way. Every time that you successfully guide a horse through a difficult or challenging situation in a fair manner, the confidence that he has in you will grow.

There are several examples in this book explaining how to work through different situations to help you better understand horses so that you can build your own horse's trust and confidence.

Communication

Communication is understanding how your horse thinks and communicates nonverbally and knowing how to communicate back to him nonverbally. You communicate with body language, energy, and emotional control and through the use of proper skills while using your reins, riding crops, spurs, whip, and other aids.

I believe that we should be willing to learn the horse's language before we try to teach them ours. If you start recognizing all the little gestures that the horse is making, you can begin to understand how the horse thinks, what bothers him, when he understands you, when he is confused, when he is trying, and when he is asking questions.

Maybe you never thought about your horse asking you a question or what that might look like. Horses often get confused when we are trying to communicate something to them. Sometimes, there is too much stimulus coming at a horse from a person's arms, legs, whips, reins, spurs, or other tools. This excess stimulus confuses him, and he is not sure what to do

sooner because you can redirect him more quickly with the lead line attached. It is best to work with a lead line until you have a clear pattern of communication with your horse that he understands. If he is facing you and you are having trouble getting his head to go to the right to start the circle to the left, point the stick or whip that is in your right hand toward his nose, and gently wiggle the stick up and down to encourage his head to turn away. Once his nose is pointed in the right direction, you can softly tap the ground behind him with the stick and string or lunge whip to ask him to go left. Once he begins traveling to the left, take all pressure off him. If he tries facing you again, keep repeating the steps until he understands. This will take some good coordination and skill on your part. It will also take patience and good control of your emotions. It is hard when you are learning and don't have all the answers. It is extremely important to your success that you stay calm, patient, and focused. If your horse is confused and you get mad at him, he will just become more confused, scared, and unconfident. Patience with yourself and your horse is very important. Once he is going to the left at the trot, leave him alone, and allow him to uphold his responsibility to maintain his gait and direction.

If you ask your horse to trot and he takes off faster than you anticipated and is being overreactive, scared, and/or unconfident, you need to figure out why. It may mean you put too much pressure on him or he does not understand the request. You may have smacked the ground too hard with your lunge whip or stick and string, you may have been too upset, or he may have just become confused. If he is frantic, wiggle the lead line up and down with rhythm so that it reaches his halter and causes him to slow down and come off his adrenaline. If he seems to get worse or does not show signs of slowing down, calming down, and being connected with you, try something different. Give him less lead line so that his circles become smaller. Small circles help the horse to calm down because he realizes that he is not going anywhere except in a small circle and because it is repetitive. You can also ask him to move his hind end away from you and to stop and face you. This can also help him to stop and reconnect with you and to begin thinking more and reacting less.

Don't try to get in front of him to stop him if he is being overreactive; a panicked horse might not be looking at you and might run right over you. There are times when the safest thing to do is to let the horse run for a few minutes until he makes the decision to slow down. In some situations, it takes lots of horsemanship skill to address a frantic horse. If you don't feel that you can manage him in this manner, please don't put yourself in a situation where you can get hurt.

The goal is to have him responsive and connected to you and not reactive and frantic. You may have some trial-and-error moments, and if one strategy does not work, try another. The answers will be different with different horses. Find what works best for your horse and your situation. Don't be afraid to experiment at the level at which you are skilled. If your strategy is bothering your horse and he is getting more worked up, you just need to try a different strategy. Work to find what helps your horse become calmer and more confident. If you run out of ideas, consider searching for a reputable trainer in the natural horsemanship field. Work hard at not getting mad at your horse. He is just trying to understand.

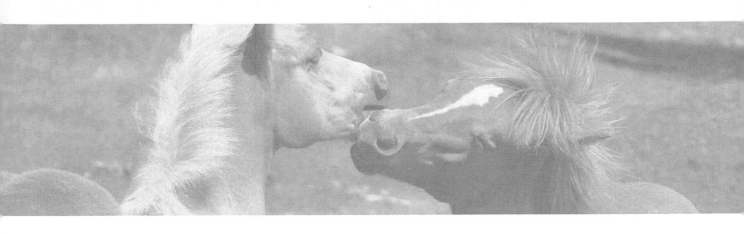

CHAPTER 16
Learned Behaviors

//

Learned behaviors are positive or negative behaviors that have developed after birth. For example, if a horse is rejected by his mother after birth, this will have a lasting effect on his behavior. If a horse is imprinted after birth, this will also have a lasting effect on his behavior. If imprinting is done correctly, it can have a positive effect, but if it is done without the proper knowledge and skill level, it may have a negative effect.

Next, I will share a personal experience about learned behaviors with you.

Behaviors That Are Learned through Life Experiences

In 2000, I attempted to imprint my first newborn foal. I understood the concept of getting the foal used to being handled and accustomed to foreign objects, so I thought that it would be easy. What I did not understand at that time was that I needed to use good timing on my release of stimulus or pressure.

I was going through the motions of rubbing the foal all over, tapping on the bottom of her hooves to prepare her for future farrier work, rubbing her with a small plastic bag, massaging her ears, and doing all sorts of things that I thought would help this foal live in the human environment. What I did not understand at that time was that I needed to pay attention to the foal's reactions to what I was doing. I should have gently continued the stimulus until the foal showed signs of relaxation. I did not understand this at the time, and I was releasing the imprinting stimulus before the foal had relaxed and accepted what I was doing. So, instead of having a relaxed and confident foal, I ended up with a foal that was worried about almost everything. That was a lesson I learned the hard way.

As the foal grows and develops, there will be many experiences that will shape how he interprets the world. The foal's dam will teach him the nonverbal horse language and what behaviors are acceptable and unacceptable. She will also teach him what to be concerned about from her perspective; this relates back to her life experiences. Learned behaviors can and do develop during all stages of a horse's life. Oftentimes, people love to spend time with foals. These young horses are often playful and exuberant, and it is fun to watch them play. People also enjoy petting them and loving on them.

Along with that playful spirit also come dominance games. People often mistake a foal's acts of dominance as playfulness. Young horses like to test their boundaries with people just as they do with their dams or other horses within a herd. You may see a foal playfully pushing his body onto a person, and the person will think it is cute and pet him. People often think that this behavior must mean that the foal loves them. Sometimes, a foal will stick his butt toward a person to get a butt scratch and will once again be rewarded with a scratch. It is cute, and it looks like fun to people, but these behaviors can be carried into adulthood, and then those same people will wonder why the horse is so rude and pushy. It is also danger-ous when a horse turns his butt toward a person; his next step could very well be a kick. The horse thinks that it is OK because he was positively rewarded for it. This behavior also makes the foal believe that he is higher in the pecking order than people because he was rewarded for his acts of dominance.

Loving on a foal is completely fine as long as it is done in a manner in which the foal learns that certain behaviors are not acceptable. Don't be mean or get mad if a foal plays dominance games. He is young and is experimenting. It is a person's job to gently teach the foal not to be pushy or push into pressure but instead to move away from pressure. Teaching a foal to move away from pressure is a skill that will benefit the foal for the rest of his life.

Tip for a Pushy Foal

When the foal approaches you and pushes his shoulder into you, gently place your fingertips on his chest area and add just enough pressure to make it too uncomfortable for him not to ignore it. Keep the pressure from your fingertips steady on his chest until he decides to take a step away from you. The moment he takes that step away, remove your fingers, and pet him for responding properly. This way, you still get to love on the foal, and he learns to not be pushy. Repeat this response on a regular basis, and he will learn to be polite and to move away from pressure as a new positive learned behavior.

Tip for a Mouthy Foal

Many foals love to nip and bite at people and other objects. The foal is experimenting with his mouth and is oftentimes teething. If the foal tries nibbling on your fingers, just keep your hand wide open with your fingers together so he can't get his mouth around your hand. If the foal is never successful at nipping, there is no benefit for him to continue nipping. If you smack him, he may become scared or head shy. He does not understand that the behavior is wrong, so just make it hard for him to take a nibble out of your hand. You can also distract the foal by causing him to move away from pressure. When he begins to nip, you can ask him to back up, move his front end or hind end away from you, or lower his head, among other things. You can visit my YouTube channel (https://www.youtube.com/user/Perigan1), which has a couple of great examples of me working with a newborn foal that is mouthy.

Pushing into Pressure versus Moving Away from Pressure

Horses are born with the instinct to push into pressure. Fortunately, we can retrain the horse's way of thinking and teach him to move away from pressure instead. If we take the time to teach him to move away from pressure instead of pushing into it, this will become a new positive learned behavior. This will take several consistent repetitions.

Let's say that you want to teach your horse to come off the pressure of the halter and walk forward with you in a positive manner. You can begin by having your horse on a halter and lead line; when you start to walk forward, the slack will come out of the lead line if the horse is not following you. Once the slack comes out of the lead line, the horse will begin to feel the pressure of the halter on his head. If the horse does not move when the lead line becomes tight, he is pushing against pressure on his pole (the area on the top of the head between the ears). The horse may become uncomfortable, and he may also raise his head in defiance or take a step backward. The horse is following his natural instinct to push against the pressure he feels from the halter.

At this point, the best thing you can do is keep the amount of pressure on the lead line the same. Do not put any slack in it. Whether he is raising his head, backing up, or just standing still, if possible, do not let the lead line become loose. It is also important to not look back at him but to instead keep looking forward. If your horse does not improve by physically taking a step forward after a few seconds, it would be a good idea to add some additional motivation. Here are a couple of suggestions:

1. You can stay facing forward while maintaining the pressure on the rope and move to either your horse's left or right. This direction change can help tip the horse off balance so that he takes a step toward you slightly to the left or right

with a front foot. When he does take a step, it is important to release the pressure on the lead rope immediately. The release of pressure will let the horse know that he has done the right thing. The release of pressure teaches the horse that whatever he did before the release was the correct answer. Remember that it will still take many repetitions to change his natural reaction to the pressure.

2. Another option is to have a stick and string or a long lunge whip with you. If the horse resists going forward, tap the ground behind him several times; this will create an additional stimulus of pressure and encourage him to take a step forward. Start with light tapping, and increase the pressure only if there is no positive reaction. Remember to stop tapping and release the pressure on the lead rope immediately when he moves forward. If he takes only a step or two and stops, all you have to do is ask again in the same manner. Keep repeating this until you have forward momentum. If there is no positive reaction, try to tap the horse lightly on the hip. Make sure the tap on the hip is gentle. You are not trying to smack him, scare him, or hurt him; you are encouraging him to move forward. If the tap on the hip is not successful, try some rhythm by adding several taps on the hip until the horse takes a step forward. It is also very important to stay calm and not get mad or upset at your horse. You are just teaching him to respond appropriately to pressure.

3. If you have an unconfident horse, you may choose to tap the ground close by his hip or behind him with the stick or whip instead of tapping him on the hip. The latter may be too much pressure for an unconfident horse. For a confident or pushy horse that is resisting pressure, the tap on the hip may encourage him to go forward. With either type of horse, it is a good idea to make sure you are not standing directly in front of him when you do add pressure. This way, if you are too firm or the horse gets scared, he will not surge forward and run into you. Safety is very important. Try different strategies, and find what works best for your horse. Always start with light pressure, and add extra pressure only if the horse is not responsive. Once he becomes repeatedly responsive to moving forward with pressure from the halter, he will have learned a new positive behavior.

If the horse learns he can resist the pressure that is put on him, he will have learned a new negative behavior. For example, let's use the same scenario: you walk forward with the lead line, and the horse does not follow. If the rope gets tight and, for any reason, you allow it to become loose before he has taken a step forward, you will have just taught him that he has done the right thing by resisting. He resisted, and the pressure came off, so he thinks that was the right answer. If you then turn around and get mad at him or smack him, it will not make sense to him. If you make a mistake and accidentally allow some slack in the line, just ask one more time, and do your best to make sure that it does not happen again. It takes only a few repetitions of a positive or negative response for it to start becoming a learned behavior, so be mindful to get the positive response you desire. If your horse has learned a negative behavior, it will take many repetitions of a positive response to replace it.

If a horse has been handled with great care from birth, his confidence will grow even if he is unconfident by nature. It may just take longer with an unconfident horse. On the other hand, if a horse has been mishandled and taught through a process of fear and intimidation, it can take a lot of work to regain his confidence and help him trust in humans. This does not mean that when you are learning and make mistakes that you will ruin your horse. We all make mistakes, and it is expected. What matters to your horse is that you teach him with love, good intentions, understanding, and fairness and that you constantly strive to learn and do better. The horse feels the intention behind your actions. This is a partnership, and he needs to be understood and treated with fairness.

CHAPTER 17
Strategies to Help You Gain Confidence with Horses

Fear is a normal, common emotion that people often feel with horses. Some people develop fear after an accident with a horse. Some people have very skittish, unconfident horses, and that brings up their own fear levels. Sometimes, it is just the fact that as we get older, we become more aware that we can get hurt, and caution and fear take a front seat in our thoughts and emotions.

Often, this is not enough to keep us away from horses because our love for them is so strong. If this sounds familiar to you, just know that you are not alone. I myself have had some traumatizing experiences that almost took my dream of working with horses away. For some reason, though, I just could not stay away from them. My love for these magnificent creatures is way too strong.

So, I did the next best thing. I became educated. I learned how to understand the horse's body language and gestures, and I learned how to communicate with the horse in a way that made sense to him. I learned how to interpret the signs that would let me know when the horse was not confident or was fearful and what I could do to teach him how to be braver and more confident. I also realized that I could learn to understand when a horse was in the right mind-set to be ridden and when he was not. When my horse is not mentally and emotionally connected with me and is not acting like a partner, I do not ride. If the horse is fearful of something, I address his concerns before I decide to ride. If my horse becomes fearful while I am riding and I don't feel I can manage the situation, I have no problem getting off and working with him on the ground until he becomes calm and confident again. After I dismount, I will work with him on a long line or lead rope, ask him to move his feet around, and ask him to perform different maneuvers and tasks until I feel that he is mentally connected to me again. If I feel I can manage his emotions while I am riding, I will do similar tasks and also add small circles to help calm him. When you have the knowledge and skills to manage these situations, your confidence grows. Whatever your fear may be, the best way to approach it is to take things slow and advance a little at a time.

Overcoming a Fear of Riding

Some people have a fear of just being able to sit on a horse. To remediate this fear, start by having the horse in a small area, such as a round pen or a stall. Start as far away from the horse as you feel is necessary to maintain a little calmness about you.

Begin approaching the horse slowly, and stay as relaxed as possible. When you feel that your emotions are starting to increase, just stop and back away momentarily. This may happen twenty feet away from the horse or right up next to the horse. It is different for everyone. It is OK wherever you are starting. Don't be hard on yourself. The idea is to gain a little confidence each time. When you feel that your emotions have calmed down, try to approach the horse again and see if you can get a little closer. When your anxiety increases, just back away, and relax again. Repeat this over and over again.

If you are at the point where you are next to the horse, offer the back of your hand to see if the horse will smell your hand. If the horse does smell your hand, try petting him on the neck and staying relaxed. There is no rush to conquer your fear. It does not have to be resolved in one session or in a dozen sessions. Do this at your own pace. If you are comfortable petting the horse, you might want to walk away for a moment just to feel a sense of achievement.

When you approach the horse again, you may want to try stretching your hand over his back where your leg would go for a moment or so, pet the horse again, and then walk away. The idea is to go just a little past where you feel comfortable each time, become accustomed to your new progress, back away, and feel a sense of accomplishment.

Your next step may be having the horse next to a fence where you can climb up, sit on the fence slightly above him, and pet him once again on the neck. I encourage you to have someone else hold the horse's lead rope so that he stays still and is under control. I also encourage you to do this with a horse that is calm by nature. This will enhance your experience and help you gain confidence more quickly.

Maybe next, you can try climbing the fence and leaning just slightly over the horse and rubbing him. Then get down, walk away for a few minutes, and feel the success of the new advancement. Next, you can try leaning the top of your body over the horse momentarily as you pet him. Keep your feet on one side so that you can slide off when you feel the need to. Repeat this step over and over until your fear subsides.

Remember, there is no rush to accomplish this task. If you do this slowly, one step at a time, there will come a point when you will want to get on the horse because you went slowly and took the time to build your confidence. When you get to the point where you are sitting on your horse, just pet him for a moment or two and then get off. Once again, repeat this as many times as you feel the need to. When you are relaxed and just sitting on his back, you can him take a step or two forward and then stop, relax, breathe, and maybe get off. Or maybe not. When you are ready and on the horse's back, try for a couple more steps, and just build on that, one piece at a time. Have someone with you that can help hold the horse so that you don't have to worry about him moving any more than you want him to.

I had a woman come to my house one day because she wanted to overcome her fear of horses. She had been badly hurt by a loose horse that had run into her years ago, and she was ready to face her fears. Before she even entered my ranch, she became terrified. She was shaking and on the verge of tears. When she got out of her car, she stayed about forty feet away from my horse Troubadour, who was in a round pen.

Troubadour was a calm, well-trained horse, and I knew he was perfect for this job. As the lady kept her distance, I played with Troubadour, and he showed off his talents as we played at liberty with lead changes, spins, and other fancy moves. Troubadour also showed how strong his bond was with me. After showing off some beautiful maneuvers with Troubadour, I slowed him down, pet him, and gently moved him around so that she could see that he was a gentle horse.

As the lady watched Troubadour and I interact, her fear subsided enough that she could get a little closer. As I continued to interact with Troubadour, she found herself getting closer and closer to him. Once in a while, she would retreat a little bit; this helped her relax. After this had gone on for about an hour, she began to relax enough that she wanted to approach Troubadour and pet him on the neck. As she was petting him, she began to sob uncontrollably, releasing a lot of her fear and anxiety. She realized that horses can be gentle and kind and that she did not need to be afraid any longer. There was a lot of healing that took place that day, and I was proud to be a part of it.

Fear of Jumping

A fear of jumping while you are on a horse is quite normal. Begin by starting with a small jump such as a ground pole. First, you can walk over the post with the horse as many times as you need to in order to feel comfortable. Then try trotting over the pole in the same manner. Once you feel confident, you may want to canter over the pole. Once you feel good with the pole, try a bigger obstacle or two or more poles placed together to add a little more difficulty to the jump. Repeat the small jumps or poles as many times as you need to in order to feel your confidence building. When each jump or pole feels easy, you are ready to move on to an ever bigger jump.

Fear of Cantering

Some people have a fear of cantering on a horse. We often think that when we are trying to conquer our fears, we need to get out there and just do it and push through our fear. It does not have to be that way. I feel it is better to take it one step at a time.

So, if you want to canter, use a horse that is comfortable with cantering, and start in a small area, such as a round pen. Make sure you are comfortable at a walk and a trot before you attempt a canter. When you are ready to try, just have the horse canter a couple of strides and then go back down to a trot or walk or stop, whatever suits you. Then slowly build on that by adding an extra canter stride or two whenever you are ready.

Before you know it, you will be cantering all around the round pen or arena. Remember, if at any time you feel a lot of fear or a loss of balance, slow down to a lower gait, and when you are ready, try again.

Confidence is gained one step at a time. To grow, you have to be willing to be a little uncomfortable. We can manage our fears and gain confidence by taking on our fears one baby step at a time.

Fearful Moments and What Often Happens in Your Body

If you ride horses, there will inevitably come a time when your horse will spook at something, buck, rear, bolt, or do something that will trigger a fear response in you. Quite often when we become afraid on a horse, we will grip with our legs, pull back on the reins, and look toward the ground; this puts us in an almost fetal position. When we look down, our anxiety and fear can increase, and we can lose touch with the reasoning side of our brain; this makes us less likely to make wise decisions. Looking down can also throw off our balance on the horse's back and make us more vulnerable to falling off or less likely to have a positive outcome. Here are some strategies you can use to help you work through these fears.

Strategy 1

One solution to this problem is to do the opposite of the behaviors I mentioned previously. If your horse gets worried while you are riding, look straight ahead, straighten your spine, and make sure your toes are up and your heels are down. This will help put you in a balance position and can also trigger your brain to think logically instead of fearfully. It will take some practice.

A good way to practice is to test yourself every time you ride and check to see whether you are looking straight ahead, your spine is straight, your toes are up, and your heels are down. Do this several times during each ride just to practice so that you begin make these motor skill responses automatic for those times when you need them. If you feel fear creeping into your thoughts, just test yourself again to make sure everything in your body is in place so that you feel more confident and safer when handling any potential fearful moments that may arise.

You can also take hold of some hair from your horse's mane and slightly pull up on it, or you can put your hand under the pommel of the saddle and pull upward. This will help you push your seat further down onto the saddle so you feel more secure.

It is also very beneficial to know how to bend your horse's head over to your knee to get him under control. This is explained in Chapter 20, "Safety Tips," under the Using a One-Rein Stop section.

Strategy 2

Another strategy that works well during a ride is to make a loud noise, such as a bang, when fear begins to creep into your thoughts. We all have negative thoughts come up in our mind from time to time, and when we are riding and we anticipate something going wrong, it can interfere with our ability to be successful. So, when this happens, yell out a loud "Bang!" This will interrupt your negative thoughts. Then quickly lift your eyes, straighten your spine, look straight ahead, and redirect your thoughts to something positive that will enhance your ride.

We do not need to let the negative noise in our head take over, ruin our confidence, and interfere with our ability to strive to do better. Sometimes, you may have to do this several times in a session, especially at first, because you need to recondition your thought process to stay in the positive. When a person starts thinking about fearful things that might happen, their eyes tend to drop, their spine bends over, and negative thoughts become consuming. So, it is important to interrupt this type of thought process as quickly as possible. If you make the "bang" noise, it interrupts it, and gives you a moment to redirect your attention. When you lift your eyes and straighten your spine at the same time, your mind becomes more open and ready to redirect and refocus positively. Then, you have the opportunity to replace the negative thoughts with more positive ones or ideas on what you can do to stay safe. At this time, it is also good to check yourself to make sure that you are sitting on the horse in a powerful position.

Before you ride, it is always a good idea to check if the horse is in a proper mind-set and not likely to buck. Once he is all saddled up, circle him at a trot or canter on a lead line, and send him over a jump a couple of times. If horses are feeling frisky or have a tendency to buck, it will often show over a jump. Change directions a couple of times as you are having the horse jump. The jumps and changes of direction will help you to see where your horse's emotions are. This can keep you safe and give him a chance to kick up his heels if he feels the need. If he is bucking over the jump, just continue to let him kick up his heels until he has lost the desire to buck. Try not to make him feel wrong for acting like a horse. Let him release his built-up energy and have fun with it. Give him what he needs, and he will be much more willing to give you what you need.

Be Mentally Prepared

When we have fearful thoughts, it not only inhibits us but also worries our horse. He picks up on our negative emotions and can see them as either a lack of leadership or a sign of potential danger. So, we really have to watch our thoughts, not only for our own benefit but for our horse's as well.

When your horse picks up on your negative emotions, you may see signs from him; he might raise his head, start looking around in a nervous manner, become very alert, and start looking for danger. The horse's body can tense up, and some horses may freeze in place and become too afraid to move. The quicker you can redirect your thoughts to positive ones, the better the ride will be for both of you.

When I redirect my attention from a scary thought to a productive one, I am training my brain to think and focus in a positive manner. So, when I redirect my thoughts, I think about what I can do to be safe instead of what might go wrong. Here is how I mentally redirect myself when I have a negative thought:

1. I focus and look straight forward.
2. I check to see whether my chin is up and my spine is straight.
3. I check to determine whether my toes are up and my heels are down.
4. I check to see if I am in a balanced position, so if my horse does spook, I can stay on.
5. I prepare to take one rein and bend the horse to a stop if needed.
6. I prepare to do an emergency dismount if needed.

Being mentally and physically prepared brings confidence. Instead of being worried about what could go wrong, I am focused and prepared to be in control and to stay safe.

When you know what to do to help you and your horse get in a good mind-set, your confidence will grow. Understanding how to approach these issues and how to work through them will help you achieve more success with horses.

These are just a couple of ideas to help you be prepared and focused in a positive way. The more knowledge you gain, the more skill you acquire, and the better you prepare yourself and your horse, the better your chances will be for a positive outcome. I truly hope I have given you some tips that will help you gain confidence and knowledge on your horsemanship journey.

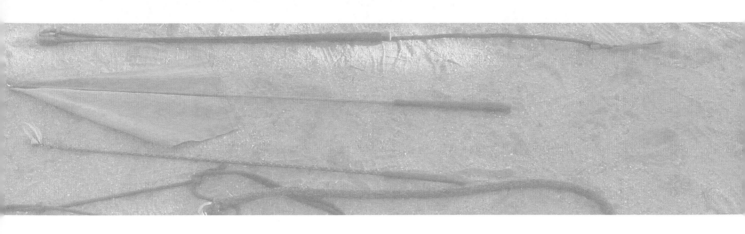

CHAPTER 18
Using Tools

//

W e want our horse to be responsive to our tools without being scared of them. It is important that we introduce the horse to these aids in a friendly way so that he does not see them as weapons or something to fear.

The tools are designed to help us influence and encourage positive responses from the horse. An object is not a tool if it is used to inflict pain or fear. There is a big difference. If a person's mind-set and approach are positive, there is a better chance of getting a positive and respectful outcome from the horse, so it is important that we learn how to use our tools appropriately.

Introducing a Lunge Whip or Stick and String to a Horse

We need to think of a lung whip or stick and string as an extension of our arm and not as a weapon to force the horse to obey. We use these tools to help us reach or influence areas around the horse where our arm cannot go.

One way to help your horse learn that the tool is not a weapon is to allow the horse to smell it and touch it with his nose and to use it to softly rub the horse's shoulder, neck, back, and legs. Once the horse is comfortable and relaxed with the tool touching his body, you can start gently swinging it around in a soft circular motion close to the ground. Make sure that your body and facial muscles are relaxed and that you are not staring at your horse. You want him to be able to tune into the sense of relaxation in your own body so that he knows that you are relaxed and calm and not asking anything of him. If you see signs of the horse becoming nervous or worried, just begin walking away from him as you gently swing the tool around and allow him to follow you. Use your peripheral vision to watch the horse, and look for signs of his curiosity to come up. When something that a horse perceives as scary begins to retreat away from him, the threatening feeling that he had will begin to dissipate, and curiosity will often take its place. Keep relaxed soft energy in your body and your face, and allow the horse to start following the tool as you are walking away from him. You can keep the tool on either your left or right side. If this task happens to take place on one side of the horse's body and the horse begins to relax and feel better about the tool, give him a few minutes to relax and process that information, and then work on the opposite side of the horse with the same task. Remember, the horse needs to see, feel, and experience the stimulus on both sides and with both eyes.

Signs That the Horse Is Scared of or Worried about the Tool

- The horse's head is high.
- His eyes are wide and unblinking.
- His nostrils are enlarged, and he may be snorting
- He is showing signs of wanting to escape or run off or is tense and unwilling to move.
- His tail is swishing quickly back and forth or is tucked between his legs.

Signs That Your Horse Is Gaining Confidence with and Curiosity about the Tool

- The horse's head is relatively low.
- He is blinking.
- There are no wrinkles around his nose, and he might be sneezing softly or smelling the tool.
- He is licking his lips or yawning.
- He is walking toward the tool on his own without tension in his body.

The moment you see any sign of improvement, you need to hold the tool still and make sure that your body energy is relaxed as well. You can even try turning your head and body to a fifteen- to forty-five-degree angle from the front of your horse so that you are not staring at him and projecting energy toward him. This will help him relax and realize that the tool is not so scary. Every time the horse makes a positive change in his body or attitude and the commotion that is being created with the tool stops, he will become calmer and braver. It is very important that you understand this concept. It is the difference between real success and mediocrity.

As your horse becomes more relaxed over a few sessions, you can increase the motion and speed of the tool a little at a time. If he gets worried, just slow down the speed to a point that he can handle. When he shows a positive sign of curiosity or relaxation, stop the motion again. Once he is OK with the tool and wants to investigate it by smelling it or trying to nibble on it, you have the green light to go ahead and softly touch him with it. Begin at the shoulder area, and rub him with it just as if you were petting him, softly and slowly. Rub a little, take it away, and then repeat. Keep doing this until you see signs of relaxation and acceptance. Slow down if the horse is worried. Watch his expressions; they will help you decide whether you should do more or less. Once he is OK with your slow progression and there are signs of relaxation and acceptance, you can rub other areas of his body with the whip or stick.

If he's raising his head and getting worried, just slow down a little. Go slowly so his confidence can grow. You may even try to swing it over his back with a gentle motion, but make sure that the end of the string or whip does not smack him. Make sure that you are at an angle to his body where he can't run you over if he becomes too afraid. If he does start heading toward you, take your hand and face it toward his eye, palm open, like a police officer stopping traffic, blocking the eye so that it looks to him as if he is going to run into it. This can be very effective. I use this technique whenever I am leading my horse around, he becomes nervous, and I feel the need to protect my space.

Once you are confident that your horse is no longer afraid of the tool, you have permission to use it to help you influence his body parts to move, but always start with bringing up energy in your body. As I mentioned before, the tool is an extension of your arm. It is to be used only if he is not responding to your request.

We don't want the horse thinking of the stick or whip as an object that causes fear and pain. We want him to view it as an extension of our hand that helps us reach further. He can learn to respect the stick or whip if we learn to use it appropriately.

Influencing Hind-End Disengagement On a Line with a Stick or Lunge Whip

Start by having your horse on a lead line and standing a few feet away from him and off to the side by his shoulder. The first step is to bring up some energy in your body by taking a good breath and stare at his hind end as if you are going to push it away with your eyes. If the horse does not begin to move his hind end away, start wiggling the lunge whip or stick gently up and down toward his hind end. If he does not respond after a couple of seconds, use the whip or stick to do a tap–tap motion rhythmically and very lightly on his hind end. If the horse still does not respond, slightly escalate the pressure of the tap–tap motion on his hind end, but stay out of his kick zone. The kick zone is the area that the horse can reach out and kick out from where he is standing. It may also help to use the hand that is closest to the horse to keep the lead rope taught, with his head slightly bent toward you. This will make it harder for him to kick toward you if he feels the need.

The moment the horse moves his hind end away, release all pressure immediately so that he understands that this is what you want. Use these steps in the same order with consistency, and your horse will learn to start responding to the slightest amount of pressure. He will understand that the pressure will escalate if he does not respond. Horses are pattern animals, and they look for patterns in everything that we do with them.

Here is the list of steps for disengaging your horse's hind end:

1. Bring up some energy in your body, and stare at the horse's hind end.
2. Gently wiggle the lunge whip or stick up and down toward the horse's hind end.
3. Use the lunge whip or stick to gently execute a tap–tap motion on the horse's hind end.
4. Slightly increase the intensity of the tap–tap motion on the horse's hind end.

It is also very important to notice when the horse is trying to figure out what you want from him and when he is just being nonresponsive. If the horse is trying, he might look as though he is a little unsure of what to do. For example, he might start shifting his weight around as if he is not sure where he should move his feet, blink irregularly or stop blinking, or raise his head slightly. If the horse is not trying, he will look as if he is ignoring you.

Watching the horse's expressions can tell you a lot about where his mind is. Being observant is a big key to success with horses.

Using a Riding Crop while You Are Riding

Before I use a riding crop to reinforce my request, I make sure the horse is not worried about it. I rub him with it on the shoulder, neck, back, legs, and sides just as if I were rubbing him with my hand. Once I am confident that there is no fear, I can use it if it is needed.

I use it if he does not respond to my body energy, seat, or legs while I am riding. Let's say that I want to ask the horse to go from a halt to a walk. The first step is to bring up some energy in my body by sitting up straight and taking a deep breath. If my horse does not respond, I gently squeeze him with my calf muscles. If he still doesn't respond, I make a smooching or clucking sound and then make a light tap–tap motion with the riding crop on his shoulder or behind his ribcage. I keep the crop vertical, and the instant the horse responds, I take off all the pressure, smile, and ride along with him.

Again, if this is a pattern and we use it with consistency and correctly, the horse will learn it and begin to respond sooner and sooner. When we apply pressure appropriately, we are fair in the way we ask, and the horse understands what we are asking, he will not be afraid or mad. He will also let us know whether we have been too firm or unfair by raising his head, pinning his ears back, kicking out, biting, or sometimes just shutting down emotionally and physically.

Here are some steps you can use to encourage forward motion or a transition of gaits:

1. Bring up your body energy.
2. Gently squeeze the horse with your calf muscles.
3. Make a smooching or clucking sound.
4. Make a light tap–tap motion with the riding crop on the horse's shoulder or behind his ribcage.

Release the pressure the moment the horse responds correctly. The quicker you can release pressure and the more you maintain a positive attitude about it, the faster the horse will learn to respond respectfully.

I always look for the attempt from the horse and for moments to reward him. That is where my focus is. The better my attention is on the moment and the better I can release the pressure, the more the horse will try. My favorite phrases are "Good boy!" and "Good girl!"

Lunge Line

A lunge line is a great tool to use when exercising a horse in a large area. You can make your circles large, small, or anywhere in between. It is a lot of fun to use the lunge line to spiral a horse from a large circle into a small one. You can slowly make the circle smaller by taking in a foot of rope at a time, and then slowly make the circle bigger until the horse is at the end of the lunge line. Exercising a horse should be about having fun and not just sending the horse out in continuous boring circles where nothing changes. So, play with the size of the circle, add some changes of gait, jumps, and poles, and use uneven ground if you can. Help the horse have fun, and engage his mind as well as his body.

Spurs

Spurs can be very handy if used properly. Spurs are not designed to spur a horse into submission or to force a horse to go forward. Spurs are not made to inflict pain on a horse in any way. They are made to encourage a horse to move away from leg pressure to the left or right. If the horse does not respond to a light use of leg pressure, a spur can be used to gently encourage him to move away from the leg pressure.

This means that the horse is not to be jabbed with the spur if he does not respond to leg pressure. Instead, offer a light touch with the spur to remind the horse that he needs to yield to the leg pressure. I don't recommend anyone using spurs until they learn not to kick the horse to go and not to squeeze tightly with the legs when the horse spooks or goes too fast. I also don't recommend them if the person can't yield and turn the horse with only light pressure from their calf muscle.

It is important that you have a good foundation on the horse and good body control yourself so the horse is never accidentally spurred. I did not use spurs until I had a solid understanding of how and when to use them, I had achieved great body position and leg position, and I had a solid foundation with my horse. Now, I use them only for gentle refinement. I believe people should have to earn the right to wear spurs.

Bridle

There is a misconception that a bridle is used to turn and stop a horse. Using a bit in this way only makes a horse feel as if he is being pulled around and micromanaged by the mouth. Often, one of the first things that a person does when something goes wrong is to get a bigger or more severe bit to try to fix the problem. The horse often gets mixed signals from the bit because there is always some form of pressure from the bit when you are turning the horse, stopping him, or riding with contact. Often, when a person rides a horse with a bit, the pressure from the use of the reins is inconsistent, and the horse never receives a release of pressure. He gets bumped in the mouth too much and does not understand what all that bumping and pulling is about. There is no consistency from a soft feel from the reins when the horse is responding appropriately or a light release or decrease of pressure when he has responded well both mentally and physically.

Riding with light contact and a steady, consistent feel on the reins is a skill worth learning. Learning to ride with your whole body, use the energy in your body to encourage the horse to be at a certain gait, and turn the horse with your body and not the reins is an art. If you take the time to learn how to properly use the bridle, the ride can become harmonious. There are some great instructors that teach people how to use a bridle in ways that make sense to the horse. Seek out good videos or DVDs from good natural horsemen and horsewomen.

The best way to stop a horse is to teach him that when your body relaxes and stops moving with him and you let out a big exhale, it is time to stop. If the horse does not stop when you stop riding, you can gently add a little pressure with the reins. The moment that the horse stops, release pressure from the reins so that the horse understands that stopping was the right answer. If you practice this skill, it will not take long for the horse to understand that when you quit riding, he can quit riding.

All our tools are aids to help us communicate with our horses in a productive manner. We ask the horse for a response to a request, and if the horse chooses not to comply, pressure is lightly applied to encourage a positive response. The pressure escalates only if the horse chooses to remain nonresponsive. The moment the horse chooses to comply, the pressure is immediately taken away.

Horses naturally understand escalations of pressure. If you were to watch a herd of horses interacting with one other, you would see moments when a more dominant horse uses escalations of pressure to encourage a more submissive horse to succumb to his request. For example, when a submissive horse tries to approach a more dominant horse and the dominant horse does not want to interact at that particular time, the dominant horse will start adding pressure toward the submissive horse. She may start by pinning her ears back. If the submissive horse proceeds further toward the dominant horse, she might pin her ears back, wrinkle her nose, and face her head toward the submissive horse. If the submissive horse still does not back away, the dominant horse may choose to bite, charge, rear, or kick out at the submissive horse. All the pressure will be taken away once the submissive horse backs off.

These are all escalations of pressure, and once the submissive horse realizes that the dominant horse will escalate the pressure the next time this happens, the dominant horse might only need to pin her ears back to encourage the submissive horse to back off. We use escalations of pressure in the same manner. We start with a request, then we add light pressure to encourage a positive response, and we escalate the pressure only if needed.

Once the horse understands that there is a pattern to our escalations of pressure, he'll be more likely to respond to the lightest amount of pressure because he knows that if he does not respond, the pressure will escalate.

It is very important that we always begin with a light form of pressure; otherwise, you will never give your horse a chance to respond to the lightest forms of pressure and will miss the opportunity to have a light horse in the future. It is just as important that we are always fair with any pressure that we put on the horse and that we maintain a calm attitude when teaching or working with the horse. Horses are masters at picking up on people's energy, emotions, and attitude. Stay calm, focused, and fair and give the horse a chance to learn. Last, don't forget to release the pressure when the horse responds appropriately.

CHAPTER 19
Plans, Patterns,
Tasks, and Body Energy

Horses Look for Patterns

It is always good to have a plan for your session with your horse and know what skills or tasks you want to improve. A plan solidifies you as the leader, gives you a focus for your time together, and is also reassuring to your horse. Make sure that your plan incorporates some patterns.

A horse needs patterns so that he can have a clear picture of what the two of you are doing. For example, let's say that you are in an arena and you decide to work on a pattern such as barrel racing for the first time. Start slowly by first walking and trotting the pattern with your horse. You are not trying to race through the pattern when you are teaching this to the horse; you are just getting him familiar with it.

After a few repetitions of the pattern, you will be surprised at how fast your horse picks it up. To the horse, it is almost like figuring out a puzzle. Horses like to understand what they are doing and why they are doing it, and patterns make sense to them. If you are randomly riding your horse around with no clear purpose and no clear pattern, he may feel lost and confused.

The pattern does not have to be complex. You can work on a figure eight pattern or on big or small circles. Transitions from one gait to another and transitions within a gait are other forms of patterns.

You may want to work on trotting for a certain number of steps and then walking for a certain number of steps. Horses can count, and if you are consistent in asking for a certain number of steps during a session and rewarding the horse when he figures it out, the horse will become mentally involved and offer more enthusiasm. This helps the horse to feel like he is an active participant in the task. It is important to always repeat a pattern until the horse understands it and starts to put some energy and effort into the pattern.

You may also want to work on more complex patterns or maneuvers, such as side passing, jumping, cutting, or improving haunches-in or shoulder-in. If you continue a pattern until there is some improvement and then quit that pattern for the session, the horse will come out feeling like a winner. Repeat the pattern on your next session, look for a small improvement again, and then quit. You will be surprised at how engaged the horse will become when he realizes that he gets to finish every session feeling like a winner. A bunch of little successes eventually add up to big successes.

When you have had some success on a pattern or task and quit that task, this does not have to mean that you have to be done spending time with your horse. It just means that you are done with that particular pattern or task. You could go on a trail ride or spend some relaxing time with your horse. Make some of your time together be just for fun. It will build great rapport.

Task: Crossing an Obstacle for the First Time

Let's say that you want to work on crossing a log in the middle of a trail, a ditch, or a stream. It does not matter what the obstacle is; what matters is setting the horse up to be successful. When you advance forward toward an obstacle, find the spot where the horse lets you know that he has approached as closely as he is comfortable. You will know this because he will stop, hesitate, back away, or become worried. At this point, you can stop for a brief moment, pet him on the neck to reassure him, and then ask him to advance a step or two further toward the obstacle. If the horse begins to advance, take all pressure off him to reward his effort. If the horse lets you know that he cannot go any further, just take a few steps backward or walk away for a few yards until he feels a little less worried. Pet him on the shoulder softly, and then go back to advancing a little bit at a time toward the obstacle. What you are trying to accomplish each time is to advance a little further than you did on the previous attempt. If the horse starts to lower his head to smell or touch the obstacle, give him some slack in the line so he can think his way through it. Every time your horse starts putting in effort, relax, take the pressure off, give him time to think, and then reward every try by retreating momentarily. If your horse does not advance any further than he did on

148

the previous try after you retreated, keep asking until there is some advancement, even if it is just an inch, then reward him again, and retreat. If he begins backing up, just let him take a few steps backward. Then ask for forward movement again, and try to advance just a little bit.

If you notice that your horse is getting more worried and the pressure seems to be too much, be flexible, and don't make the task more important than building the horse's confidence. This is not about getting over or past the obstacle at any cost. If you have the mind-set that an obstacle is just an opportunity to help the horse build his confidence, you will begin to approach obstacles in a way that helps him to learn and his confidence to grow. Allow the horse time to think and assess. You may find that when the horse becomes worried, you put too much pressure on him, get mad, push too hard, or rush through the process. It is tough when you are learning and you do not have the experience to know exactly when to ask, how much to ask, and when to retreat and reward. It is OK to take a break and reassess.

If the horse is pushed too hard to get to the other side of the obstacle and he does it fearfully, he will not have gained anything. He will not be better at it the next time you ask him to cross an obstacle. If he crosses the obstacle calmly with his head low at a relaxed walk, he is showing you that he has gained confidence.

Sometimes, he will need to cross the obstacle many times before he can do it calmly. Sometimes, he will rush through the obstacle the first time or two, and that is OK. Just take a few steps away and then turn around, stay calm, and ask the horse to cross the obstacle again. Look for signs of improvement. The task will not be complete until the horse can cross the obstacle in a calm and confident manner. So, take the time that your horse needs to build his confidence.

Signs That the Horse Is Trying

- The horse lowers his head.
- He is blinking.
- He is smelling the object or the ground close to it, sneezing softly, and breathing softly.
- He is licking his lips.
- He is pawing at the ground. (This can show either trying or frustration, so watch for other signs.)

Signs That the Horse Is Afraid or Worried

- The horse's ears are tight and tense or are flickering around a lot.
- His eyes are wide and unblinking.

- His nostrils are flared, and he might be snorting.
- His head is high.
- He is walking or backing away.
- He is pawing at the ground aggressively.
- He can't stand still and can't go forward.

Signs That You Are Taking Pressure Off the Horse

- You have stopped all movement of your whip, stick, or lead line.
- Your eyes are soft.
- You are smiling.
- You are verbally letting your horse know that you are pleased.
- Your breathing is relaxed.
- Your shoulders are relaxed.
- There is slack in the reins or lead line.
- If you are on the ground, your body is turned slightly away from the horse at a ten-o'clock or two-o'clock position.

Task: Teaching a Horse to Stand on a Pedestal

When teaching a horse to stand on a pedestal, you can use the same techniques that I have described for helping a horse to cross an obstacle. You can do this while you are riding or have the horse on a lead line as you ask the horse to approach the pedestal. If your horse stops right before the pedestal and wants to smell it or paw at it, that is OK. If your horse has stopped smelling and pawing at the obstacle, walk him away from the pedestal for a moment or two, and keep a feeling of relaxation in your own body. You are not trying to pressure your horse onto the pedestal; you are helping him gain confidence to do something that might be frightening to him. Next, reapproach the pedestal, and try again. You are not looking for the horse to stand on the pedestal right away; you are just asking him to advance a little closer or put one foot on it. Even if your horse takes the foot off right away, that is OK. It is still progress. If, during your next attempt, the horse keeps one foot on the pedestal for a longer period of time or puts two feet on the pedestal, let him know that he has done a good job, and walk away with him. Keep up this pattern of asking for just a little more, and once your horse begins to try, take all the pressure off, give him time to think, and when he shows effort, walk away to reward him. If he gets to the point where he puts all four feet on the pedestal but gets right off, that is OK. Just reward him for trying and then ask again. For unconfident horses, this might take longer, so you need to show more patience and stay calm. This does not have to be accomplished in one day or one session. If it is accomplished in one session, that is good, but don't put that pressure on you or your horse. It just sets you both up to fail.

If you get frustrated or mad, your horse can feel your disappointment. When you relax and reward the horse's every try and you don't blame him for being skeptical, he will feel your approval. The goal is to make some positive progress one baby step at a time. If you find that your horse is getting worried and that progress has stopped, take a moment to assess the situation. This may mean that you need to slow down and give the horse time to think. It is OK to take a break and try again later. Confidence can't be rushed.

Body Energy: Advanced Lunge-Line Challenge Using Your Body Energy to Improve Communication and Effort from Your Horse

Let's say that you want your horse to do a twenty-meter circle on a lunge line. When you ask your horse to go, consistently use a series of cues so that the horse understands that if he does not respond right away, more cues or phases of pressure will follow. The first thing to do is to bring up some energy in your body by taking a deep breath and standing tall and proud. The next cue is to take your hand with the lunge line and gently point your finger in the direction that you want the horse to go. If the horse is already facing a certain direction, you can set him up for success by asking the horse to go in that direction. Have a specific gait, such as the trot, in mind. If the horse complies with the request, relax your body, breath normally, and smile. Have in mind how many laps you would like the horse to travel, and don't ask for too many in the beginning, maybe two to four.

Allow the horse to continue in a circle with you standing still in the center. Stay still and relaxed as long as he maintains the gait and direction you have asked for. If he breaks gait or changes direction, just calmly ask again in the same manner. Don't correct the horse or add more pressure if he is successfully fulfilling your request. If you put additional pressure on him or maintain pressure after he starts to trot, he has no way of knowing that he is doing what you want. The horse is going to understand that he is doing the right thing only if you take all pressure off, both emotional and physical, the moment he responds correctly.

If the horse does not go into a trot when you ask, you can add more cues in a sequential order. Give the horse a couple of seconds to respond to your request with your first cue of bringing up your body energy and gently pointing your finger in the direction you want him to go. If the horse does not respond after a couple of seconds, add rhythmic pressure from a stick and string or a lunge whip by gently tapping the ground behind him three or four times in a row. Remember to use light taps and not to whack the ground hard. Tapping is a consequence with good intentions behind it. Whacking comes with more force and negative emotion, and the horse knows the difference.

There has to be a sequence of phases of pressure for the horse to realize that if he does not respond to the lightest cue, there will be additional cues of pressure to come. If you begin this way, you will end up with a horse that becomes lighter and softer with his response as time goes on. Always start with the lightest amount of pressure from your cue and increase it only if the horse is nonresponsive. If you have a more sensitive horse, starting with very light pressure is important. You can ask a sensitive horse to go out on a twenty-meter circle in the same manner as a confident horse but with much less pressure.

If the horse is confused, slow down, and make sure he understands what you are asking. If he is overreactive, he probably became scared, and you will need to use less pressure next time. If your horse is nonresponsive or sluggish, you may need to do some trouble-shooting. You may need to figure out if he is bored from too much repetition, if there a lack of understanding, leadership, or respect, or if the horse is in pain. There can be lots of reasons for confusion or reactivity. Sometimes, getting help from a knowledgeable natural horseperson can do a world of good. There is no one answer for every problem. Every situation is unique, and understanding your horse from his point of view is key to having a good partnership.

It is important to make circling your horse on a long line intriguing for your horse by having the circling area on uneven ground, transitioning between gaits or speed, or including poles or jumps to make it more fun. Also, don't do so many circles that you drive your horse crazy. If the horse is light and responsive, stop and do something different. If you stop when the horse is responsive and attentive to you, he will feel good about the task. If you do the task so long that he loses enthusiasm, the horse will become dull.

Body Energy: Changing Gaits by Using Your Body Energy while You Are Riding

Horses are very good at tuning into the energy level that your body is exerting during a ride. Let's say that you are riding your horse at a walk, and you would like him to trot. Instead of kicking him to go, try to bring up the same amount of energy in your body that you would use if you were trotting on your own two feet and take a good deep breath and smile. This may be hard at first, but keep trying. If your horse does not respond, try squeezing a little with your calf muscles. If that does not work after a couple of seconds, smooch or cluck, and keep the leg pressure on. If he still has not responded after a couple more seconds, use a riding crop to gently tap him on the shoulder or behind the ribcage with a consistent soft tap–tap–tap rhythm while still keeping your energy up and your legs on him. The moment he begins to trot, take all pressure off from your aids, but keep your energy up and smile. If you repeat this series of steps in the same order every time, he will begin to see the pattern and will soon respond to just the energy that you bring up in your body. If he breaks gait, just ask again in the same manner.

When you first begin this process, it will take some time for your horse to understand exactly what it is that you are asking, especially if he has a history of being kicked and whacked to go. With consistent repetition, he will understand the new pattern. Once he understands and begins to respond to the energy that you bring up in your body, the resistance that he used to have will change, and the horse will respond more quickly and with a much more positive attitude.

Here are the four steps again:

1. Bring up energy in your body, breathe in, and feel positive.
2. Gently squeeze the horse with your calf muscles.
3. Make a smooching or clucking noise.
4. Lightly tap the horse with your riding crop on his shoulder or behind his rib-cage with a soft, consistent rhythm.

Plan on having about two seconds between each of these four cues so the horse can understand the pattern. When your horse does trot, you want your lower body from the hips down to move in harmony with his movement. Just follow the movement of your horse or post the trot by only lightly touching the saddle with your seat, and you will feel more harmonious. If you sit too hard in the saddle while posting the trot, it is hard on the horse's back and can cause him to raise his head high and hollow his back. This makes it hard to stay in rhythm.

If you want your horse to slow down to a walk again, bring the energy in your body down slightly to the amount of energy you would have if you were walking on your own two feet, change your body rhythm to a walking motion, and breathe a little more slowly. If the horse does not slow down to a walk, you can gently ask by raising up one rein. The moment the horse walks, release the pressure on the rein so he knows that he has done the right thing. Remember to keep walking energy in your body.

Do the same thing if you want him to stop. First, take the walking energy out of your body by exhaling, stopping your own riding motion, relaxing your body and legs, and slowing your breathing. If he does not respond, gently raise one rein until the horse stops, then release the pressure on the rein, and pet him. Eventually, he will learn to respond to just the energy in your body.

Whether you are trying to speed up or slow down, the energy in your body can greatly enhance your riding experience. This change in energy and his response can also begin to look like a dance between you and your horse. He will also be much happier that you are part of the dance.

Here are the steps for slowing down or stopping:

1. Slow your breathing down.
2. Change your body rhythm to a lower gait or stop the riding motion in your body.
3. Gently ask for the horse to slow down or stop by raising up one rein.
4. Release the rein pressure the moment the horse responds.

Visualization

Visualization can also play a big role in the amount of success you have with your horse. If you have a mental picture of the task at hand and you can see each step in your mind as you are executing it, it will help you and your horse stay more focused. Be clear, use patterns, use your body energy, have a picture in your mind, and be focused on the present moment, and your results will improve.

Some tasks may take only a few moments to accomplish, and some others may take days, weeks, or longer. This will depend on your level of savvy and experience and on the horse's level of confidence and his trust in you. The idea here is to advance at a pace that is good for that particular horse. Watching for signs that he is trying and knowing when it is time to reward his efforts will play a big role in your horse's confidence and development. You can learn this through practice and trial and error or by seeking out a reputable natural horseperson. I suggest having an instructor or trainer who can mentor you. My own mentors were crucial to my development and success.

CHAPTER 20
Safety Tips

I t is a good idea to have some strategies in mind to help you stay safe in the event that your horse becomes scared, spooked, panicky, or just disrespectful. Take the time to practice safety maneuvers until they become automatic responses. When a safety maneuver or any other maneuver that you want to learn is not practiced regularly, there is a good chance that you will not be equipped to use it when you really need it. If you have to take the time to think about what you should do, your timing will be late, and there is a greater chance that things will go wrong. Safety maneuvers that have become habit will add to your confidence because you will be equipped to handle emergency situations. Here are some ideas that may come in handy for you.

Stay Out of Your Horse's Kick Zone

One of the horse's defense mechanisms is to kick out at someone or something if he is worried or has a problem. There are several reasons that a horse might kick. For example, you were walking behind him without him being aware of your presence, he feels that you were unfair by putting too much pressure on him, he is fighting for food rights, or he is attempting to gain a dominant position. Whatever the case may be, it is good practice to stay out of a horse's kick zone when you are actively doing something with him. If you have to do something within the kick zone area, such as grooming the horse or cleaning his feet, stay cautious of his mood and behavior so that you stay safe.

Whenever you are standing on the ground and requesting a maneuver from a horse, make sure that you stay safe and at a distance that keeps you from getting kicked. If you know that the horse has a kicking distance of about seven feet, stand twelve feet away. Your horse kicking out at you is feedback from him letting you know that there is a problem. Oftentimes, the horse shows signs before a kick, such as pinning his ears back or wrinkling his nose, sharply swishing his tail, or giving a nasty look, that the person does not see. Being observant goes a long way in helping keep you out of trouble with your horse.

If the horse is on a lead line and you feel that you have put yourself too close to his back feet, you can always bend his head toward you so that he can either move his hind end away or bring his front end toward you. He will have a hard time kicking you if he is facing you.

Handling Your Horse on a Line

It is a good idea to allow at least two to four feet of lead line between the halter and where your hand holds the lead line. I suggest a lead line that is at least ten feet long. When horses are worried, the worst thing you can do is hold the lead line closer to where it attaches to the halter. The horse starts feeling claustrophobic and restricted from movement, and this intensifies his emotional state. Horses don't like to feel trapped, and they often need some freedom of movement to calm down and relax. In the wild, if a horse is worried, he may choose to run a short distance and then stop to reassess the situation. Allow the horse some slack in that line so that he can feel the freedom of movement. You are less likely to have a horse run into you or step on you if he has some freedom of movement. If you know some groundwork skills, you can direct where his feet go. You can have the horse change directions several times, back him up, send him over jumps, ask for some small circles, and so on. Try different maneuvers, and see what works best. If you feel unsafe and unable to manage the situation, it is best to put the horse back in a stall or pasture until you can get help and seek more solutions.

Teach Your Horse to Respect Your Space while He Is on a Lead Line

When you are walking your horse on a lead line, it is a good idea to teach him to respect your space and maintain a distance that is comfortable for you. This can keep you safe when the horse decides to spook or if he is just acting pushy.

Start by walking or leading your horse toward your destination. Practice stopping periodically along the way. When you stop, you also need to relax the muscles in your body and exhale. If your horse does not stop immediately when you stop and instead runs into you or your personal space, you need to do something about it. You need to let him know that running into you or bumping into you is not an option. You will be much safer if you have a good automatic response in place. Here is an idea that may help you. If your horse is behind you and you stop but your horse does not respond or stop when you do, stand still, and try to do a backward kick with the heel of your foot toward your horse's chest, or you can swing a riding crop or stick backward toward his chest. You do not need to do this with a lot of force; just use gentle firmness. Start by making a light tap–tap on the chest with the stick. If the horse raises his head and stops blinking, do not add additional pressure with the tap–tap. Just maintain the taps until the horse makes an effort to back up. If the horse is getting more worried, decrease the intensity of the tapping. If the horse is ignoring you and his head is relatively low, increase the intensity of the tap–tap motion to encourage a response. Also, make sure that you let the rope slide through your hand so that when your horse backs up, you don't stop him because the lead rope is too tight. It is important to continue adding intensity to that tapping with the stick or the backward kicking until you get at least a little response from your horse and he takes at least one step backward. If you quit before he backs up at least one step, he will think he was right by not moving away. Once again, the horse knows that when you release pressure, whatever he just did was the right thing whether or not it was the action you desired.

The rearward kick is one way that horses communicate with one another. An alpha horse will kick out at a less dominant horse to let him know that he needs to keep out of her space. This usually gets the other horse's attention right away. Once your horse takes a step backward, stop and stand still, with your body relaxed and your energy soft. This will usually get his attention, he will start focusing on what you are doing, and he will start staying out of your space. If your horse is more sensitive, put less pressure on him. If you are not sure, start with a small amount of pressure because you can always add more pressure if needed. If you add too much pressure and he panics and takes off, just calmly retrieve your horse, pet him, and make a mental note to be lighter with your pressure next time. Remember to relax your body when the horse responds appropriately. You can do this by exhaling and softening your shoulders and your facial expression. If you stop but your energy is still high or you feel excited or mad, your horse may get confused.

Another option is to have a stick and string or a whip with you and, if the horse is not respecting your space, to start swinging it up and down or swing it in a circular motion in front of the horse so that if he does not stop, he will run into the stick or whip. Don't go after the horse with it; let him feel as if he ran into it because he did not stop. It usually does not take many repetitions of this for the horse to get the idea that when you stop, he needs to stop. The moment the horse stops his feet, remember to stop the action of the stick or whip.

Dealing with a Loose Spooked Horse

If you find yourself in a situation where there is a loose horse running in your direction, it is good to know how to protect yourself. Here are a few ideas that you can practice:

- If possible, get out of the way or stand behind a solid object.
- Make yourself look bigger by swinging your arms up and down or doing some jumping jacks.
- Make loud noises to get the horse's attention. You can yell or slap your hands together.
- If you have something in your hand, wave it around. It can be a piece of clothing, a lunge whip, a clipboard, or any object.

Using a One-Rein Stop

The one-rein stop is an important safety skill for stopping your horse successfully when he becomes spooked, flighty, or fearful. This requires that you teach your horse to bend his neck around far enough for his head to reach your leg above your knee on either side. When he learns this technique and he is light and responsive at the halt, teach it at the walk, trot, and canter. Pulling with two reins can actually give power to the horse instead of taking it away. Bending your horse's nose to your leg will take away his ability to go anywhere, except maybe in a small circle. You also need to practice this procedure enough times that it becomes an automatic response you can use when the moment arises. Our natural instinct when a horse becomes afraid and takes off is to squeeze with our legs and pull back with both reigns. This gives the horse mixed signals: go and stop. Plus, the horse will feel your fear, which validates his feeling of fear and his need to bolt.

Teaching a horse to bend his head from side to side may take some time if he is used to resisting pressure. The best way to start is to teach him to yield to pressure. Let's say that you want to start with him bending his head to the left. Slide your left hand down the left rein until there is no slack left in it. Begin to close your fingers slowly, and start asking him to turn his head to the left. Don't pull hard; just ask the horse to bend his head a small amount to the left. If he braces against the rein, just maintain the pressure until he bends just a little bit to the left, and then release the pressure on the rein immediately. Repeat this several times until the horse begins to bend his head to the left more quickly and with less pressure from the rein. He will learn that it is the right response when he feels the release of pressure, but it may take repetition to override his natural instinct to brace. You need to release the pressure for only a moment or two and then ask again. At

first, just ask for a little bit of a bend in the neck and head to the left, and gradually ask for more and more bend until he can bend all the way to your knee. This will also help you to begin to formulate a new response and reaction to flighty moments. When you are teaching this, practice while the horse is standing still and until you feel the horse understands it. Also, remember that whatever you practice on one side of the horse, you have to practice on the other. Get him bending well on both sides, and then you can begin to practice at a walk and eventually a trot and a canter. When you practice at a walk, a trot, and eventually a canter and you bend his head to one side, look for him to stop and bend his head. The goal is for him to bend his head around, stop, and relax. Once he stops, make sure he is relaxed and not braced against the rein before you release it. When you begin to add motion and speed to a task, it often becomes more difficult for the horse, and more resistance may show up. This is normal, and you will have to patiently work through it. The better your timing is on the release of pressure, the faster it will go. If you have just added in the walk, trot, or canter to the exercise and find that your horse is more resistant, braced, or worried, just understand that this is normal. Practice this at one gait over many sessions, and eventually, your horse will be able to do this exercise at all gaits with no bracing or resistance.

Emergency Dismounting

Emergency dismounting skills are helpful for keeping you safe and able to dismount from your horse before potential disaster strikes. First, you need to be able to take one rein and bend your horse's head to one side, just as I explained with the one-rein stop in the last section. It is so important to teach your horse to flex his neck to either side and be relaxed. I will explain how to do the emergency dismount on the left side of the horse, but it can be done on either side.

Begin by having the horse's head bent to the left with the left rein in both hands. Take both feet out of the stirrups, keep the rein in your left hand, and put that hand on the horse's neck. Put your right hand a little lower on the horse's neck, swing your right leg over to the left side of the horse, and land on the ground with your feet parallel to your horse. Keep your eyes up and focused on the horizon. This will help keep your body centered and balanced.

If you feel that your horse might get worried about your dismounting in this manner, practice getting on and off your horse in a normal manner several times until your horse is calm about it. When you step off the horse, keep the rein in at least one hand so if he startles, he will run into the pressure of the bit or halter, and this should cause him to turn and face you. Practice this often so that it becomes an automatic response if you ever feel the need to get off the horse in a hurry.

I can't count how many times I have used this technique both in practice and when I have felt the need to dismount quickly. It is great for keeping your confidence intact. It is better to get off when the horse becomes worried or unconfident and find it to be a false alarm than to not get off until it is too late, and you fall off instead. There is no shame in dismounting from your horse should you become concerned for your safety.

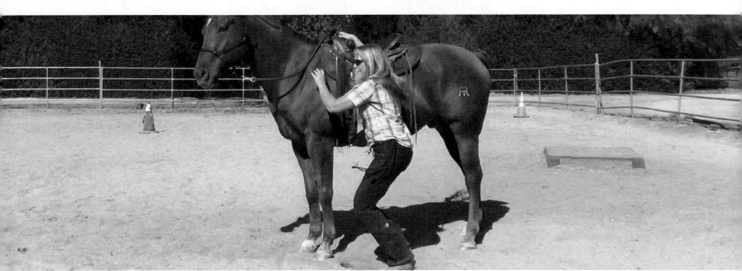

Important Note

If your horse happens to be skittish around his hind end or with motion anywhere around his body, you should address this before practicing emergency dismounts, so if you accidentally bump him with your foot on the butt, he does not spook. Get your horse used to objects and stimuli moving around his hind end and his whole body.

There are many different strategies that can help you stay safe. These are just a few that I feel may help and that I practice and use. Remember, there are some very good trainers that can help you on your journey. You just have to be particular about whom you choose, and make sure you feel comfortable with their teaching techniques. If you choose a trainer and their methods don't feel right to you, move on to another. Trust your gut, and it will guide you in the right direction. If you become a safe and confident rider, it will help your horse believe in your leadership skills, and it will improve your partnership.

Closing

////////////////////////////////

I want to thank you for taking time to read this book. I hope you have gained some insight into horse behavior and what is important to the horse from his point of view. Learning to communicate with horses can be a positive and powerful endeavor when it is done correctly. It takes time and persistence to be able to understand how horses communicate with one another and to learn to see and understand horses' nonverbal communication, but this is attainable for anyone willing to put in the work. When communication is shared and understood between you and your horse, a two-way conversation takes place, and this is where your dreams begin to become possible.

Understanding that every horse has his own individual personality will help you to personalize your sessions with your horse in a way that is appropriate for him. You want your horse to be able to be calm and in a learning frame of mind, but for that to happen, you have to meet the horse where he is emotionally and mentally. When you are able to observe the horse and understand his nonverbal language, you will be able to respond appropriately and help him be successful.

With horsemanship, sometimes we are the teachers, and sometimes we are the students. We have a lot to gain if we can be humble enough to realize that the horse has so much to teach us. We just have to be willing to listen with our eyes and our heart. There is not one of us that has all the answers to horsemanship. Sometimes, we have to dig deep to find solutions to our horsemanship challenges. Choose strategies that feel good in your heart. If they do not feel right to you, they will not feel right to the horse.

It is also amazing to find out how much our emotions and body language affect the horse. The horse has the ability to recognize when we are happy, pleased, sad, angry, or frustrated.

Our positive emotions help the horse to feel good and successful. Our negative emotions can put him on alert, and he will respond as if he is in danger. If you can leave all those negative emotions behind before you approach your horse, he will be a much better horse around you. A student of mine hung a sign up at her barn that said, "No trash talk at the barn." It reminds her to stay positive while she's around her horses.

Last but not least, knowing that the release of pressure is the way to show the horse that his action is correct is a huge key to success. Be consistent with the way you apply pressure or phases of pressure, and always start with the lightest amount of pressure possible. Offering a release of pressure when the horse is positively responsive gives the horse the information that he needs to be successful.

Horsemanship is a lifelong endeavor. Keep learning, be patient with yourself and your horse, and never be afraid to seek help when you have run out of ideas. The dreams that you have for yourself and your horse can come true. Keep believing, be humble, and reward your horse every chance you get.

Made in United States
North Haven, CT
14 August 2022

22736092R00096